Grace Under Pressure

A Story About Leadership and the Hidden Cost of Ambition

Shae Bynes

Grace Under Pressure: A Story About Leadership and the Hidden Cost of Ambition

Copyright © 2025 by Shae Bynes.

All rights reserved. No part of this publication may be reproduced, distributed, or transmitted in any form or by any means, including photocopying, recording, or other electronic or mechanical methods, without the prior written permission of the publisher, except in the case of brief quotations embodied in critical reviews and certain other noncommercial uses permitted by copyright law. For permission requests, write to the publisher at the address below.

Published by Kingdom Driven Publishing

4846 N. University Drive #406

Lauderhill, FL 33351

Disclaimer:

This allegory is a work of fiction. Names, characters, businesses, places, events, and incidents are either the products of the author's imagination or used in a fictitious manner. Any resemblance to actual persons, living or dead, or actual events is purely coincidental.

ISBN: 978-0-9996763-6-3

Printed in the United States of America

First Edition

To contact the author about speaking to your audience of leaders or employees, please visit ShaeBynes.com.

Contents

Acknowledgments 1

Foreword 3

Chapter 1: Ascending Vision 5

Chapter 2: Fuels for Greatness 15

Chapter 3: Obsession 25

Chapter 4: Whispers of Truth 33

Chapter 5: Fractured Ambition 41

Chapter 6: Burning Questions 49

Chapter 7: Wings of Stillness 53

Chapter 8: Beneath the Surface 61

Chapter 9: The Push and the Pull 71

Chapter 10: The Tipping Point 77

Chapter 11: The Countdown 89

Chapter 12: Truth on Trial 101

Chapter 13: A Line in the Sand 109

Chapter 14: Epilogue 117

The Invitation 123

About The Author 131

Acknowledgments

I've authored and co-authored many books for business owners, but this is the only one that was a dream in my heart for years before it was ever written. A seed was planted in 2018 when I read my fourth book in The Go-Giver series by Bob Burg and John David Mann, titled *The Go-Giver Influencer: A Little Story About a Most Persuasive Idea*. I thought to myself, "One day, I'm going to write a fiction story for business owners." Seven years later, that dream was birthed. Thank you, Bob and John, for the inspiration!

Grace Under Pressure was shaped and strengthened by the contributions of many individuals.

To those who helped refine and elevate this book: Steve Gandara, Kim Avery, Nadia Brown, Audra Thompson, Matt Wilson, Preston Ward, and Andrew Simpson. Your insights, feedback, and support were invaluable in making this story more impactful.

To the ones who were instrumental in bringing this book into existence: Dr. Karen Maxfield, thank you for our confirming conversation over lunch in Dallas. Allen Arnold, your coaching gave me the clarity and confidence to take this vision and make it a reality. Cynthia Austin Tucker, thank you for your meticulous eye and editing assistance.

To my husband and best friend, Phil Bynes, thank you for always supporting my work and encouraging me every step of the way.

And finally, to the thousands of readers of *Grace Over Grind* — the foundation upon which *Grace Under Pressure* is built — your receptivity to the message and your feedback over the years fueled me during my writing process.

Thank you, thank you, thank you, and God bless you all!

Foreword

I first met Shae Bynes at a gathering in Texas hosted by a mutual friend. At the time, I knew she had a heart for transforming lives and businesses, but I had no idea how deeply her work would impact me in the following months. Her book *Grace Over Grind: How Grace Will Take Your Business Where Grinding Can't* was game-changing for me. I was delighted to hear that she was writing this current work as an allegory that would bring some of the key principles from *Grace Over Grind* to life in a fresh new way.

At my company, Excellent Cultures, we often speak of the "Culture Monster"—a dark force lurking beneath the surface of every company. He's the dark side of every human being that comes out due to stress, exhaustion, selfish ambition, and frustration. Without the right tools for discovery and transformation, it can erode even the best intentions. *Grace Under Pressure* demonstrates this concept well, providing a vivid look at organizational dynamics while offering insight into the real struggles leaders face in high-performance work environments.

Every great story invites us to see ourselves in its pages, challenging us to consider new perspectives and often to confront truths we've long avoided. *Grace Under Pressure* is no exception. The story's characters reflect the experiences of business leaders I've worked with for nearly five decades, yet Shae's book goes beyond highlighting these challenges; it reveals a path forward for navigating them with clarity.

Read with an open heart and mind. The lessons within have the power to transform your leadership, your organization, and your life.

Steve Gandara

Co-Founder and Managing Director

Excellent Cultures

CHAPTER 1

Ascending Vision

Every inch of this place screams success, Grace thought to herself as the glass doors automatically opened and then shut behind her.

She stood for a brief moment, taking in the scenery that surrounded her daily. VirtuPath Inc.'s meticulous design, with its shiny floors and walls filled with inspirational art, was familiar, yet even after seven years, it still spoke to her in new ways. She looked over at the massive purple sign — "Always Forward. Always Virtu." — that practically covered an entire wall and smiled to herself. *"Yes. Gotta keep movin' forward."*

VirtuPath was well-known for its products that acknowledge achievement and foster ambition — trophies, wall plaques, prints, and award badges. Grace Stillman was three years into her role as department manager, leading the team that produced the EverAscend™ premium award badges. Out of VirtuPath's 52 employees, the EverAscend team was one of the smallest teams in the company, yet it generated the highest net revenue across all product lines. After spending 16 months taking night classes to finish her master's in Strategic Management and Executive Leadership, she was ready to put what she learned into action with her team, filled with creative marketing, sales, and product development rockstars. They were doing well, but there was still plenty of opportunity for growth.

Grace enjoyed her work and believed in VirtuPath's mission: "Elevating Lives, Recognizing Achievement. Because Every Milestone Matters." Although she wasn't the Founder or CEO, she consistently envisioned VirtuPath's future and saw herself and her two children, Mia and Caleb (ages 17 and 13), as a significant part of it.

Grace could already see their fingerprints on VirtuPath's future, as if they were part of its very DNA. Mia, with her sharp eye for detail and passion for design, had been sketching product concepts since middle school, filling notebooks with logos, badges, and creative award ideas. Grace couldn't help but smile as she recalled Mia showing her a sleek new badge design over breakfast last month, saying, "Mom, people don't just want to achieve things; they want something beautiful to remember it by."

Then there was Caleb—forever curious, quick to ask questions that no one else thought to ask. Where Mia saw the art, Caleb saw the mechanics, fascinated by how things worked and why people valued them. "Who decides which achievements are worth celebrating, Mom?" he'd asked her once while fixing the hinge on his bedroom door, completely unfazed by its weight. Grace had laughed at the time, but his question lingered with her. Caleb would thrive on the strategy side of the business someday—digging into market needs and helping build systems that made achievement accessible to more people.

"*Always Forward. Always Virtu,*" she thought again, feeling a sense of quiet pride. It was more than just a slogan. It was a foundation for the future—for her, for her kids, and for what was possible. She didn't need them to follow her path, but if they wanted to be part of VirtuPath, she knew they'd bring something unique to the table.

"I can't wait to buy this business one day. I know Victor is getting tired, and there's so much more we can do."

Grace dropped off her jacket and bag in her office and hustled over to the Summit conference room for the daily team huddle meeting that was starting in five minutes.

The air seemed almost electric as she walked through the sleek hallways. There was tension in the atmosphere, but it carried an aspirational energy. She stopped momentarily to review The Pinnacle Wall, which showcases VirtuPath's most iconic EverAscend badge designs. Her favorite ones were the limited-edition badges because they reminded her of the special moments they created for some of her favorite clients. Last year, the team created custom badges for their family business clients who had successfully transitioned leadership from one generation to the next. They also created a Savvy Solutionist Badge inspired by a senior vice president at a long-time client firm to honor a scientist who solved a problem they'd been struggling with for five years.

"*Completely worth all the hard work,*" Grace thought to herself.

She turned the corner and entered the Summit conference room. Four of the six team members were already seated comfortably in their ergonomic chairs. Coffee cups, protein bars, and bags of trail mix cluttered the table.

"Good morning, team! Happy Wednesday. I see you're already ready to go. I'm sure Brandon and Tori will be here shortly. John, let's go ahead and get this party started."

John, the team's head of marketing, pressed the red button on the side of the conference table. A digital screen rose smoothly into view, displaying the week's metrics, deadlines, and upcoming goals.

Brandon, one of the sales managers, walked in—a coffee cup in one hand and a company-issue tablet in the other. "Sorry I'm late, guys." He held up his cup. "I'm already on my third cup and it's only 9:05 a.m. Natasha, you're our head designer. Quick...make me a Java Champion badge."

Natasha rolled her eyes and laughed. "Next thing you know, we'll be competing for a 'Most Jittery' trophy."

Tori walked into the conference room and immediately sat in her chair. "Sorry for my tardiness, y'all. One of my Instagram posts from yesterday went crazy, and I got caught up responding to comments. Over 300 new followers from that one photo of Angela and Brandon wearing those gigantic badge costumes. Angela's got influencer energy, while Brandon's giving 'deer in headlights'—but hey, the audience loves both. We'll have to do an EverAscend fashion show and make some reels from it."

The team laughed as Grace walked to the head of the table next to the digital screen.

"Good stuff, team! Alright, we need to get this meeting started so we can all get going. Plus, I have a meeting with Victor after this. Everyone, take a look at this board. I know it's been an intense week, but your hard work is paying off. We have already reached our monthly sales goal, and we still have another week left. That's huge!"

Brandon leaned back with a satisfied grin and raised his coffee cup like a toast. "Here's to us—EverCaffeinated and EverAscending!"

Grace continued, "As great as our sales numbers are, the good news doesn't end there. Our marketing engagement is up 32%, thanks to John and Tori's campaigns."

John and Tori gave each other a high five, and John said, "We definitely had some late nights the past two weeks, but it was worth it."

Craig raised an eyebrow at John, "Late nights, bro? You made that sound like it was unusual. That's my regular rhythm these days. Natasha, you might need to give me that Java Champion badge too!"

The team chuckled.

Natasha said, "I think I really need to get that one designed. I'm sure our customers will love it, and surely, our entire team has earned it in the past couple of months. It's all good. The coffee grind is fueling our performance grind!"

Grace tapped the digital screenboard to reveal her first announcement.

"Speaking of badges, I have a couple of announcements. This is exciting company-wide news that I'm finally able to share with you. Introducing," Grace said with a dramatic pause, "our exclusive VirtuPath Employee Achievement badges! These badges have been part of a secret project that Victor has been working on for months. I didn't even know about it until last week."

The team jokingly "ooooh" ed and "aaaahhh" ed before leaning in to hear more. They loved joking around, but they loved the idea of Employee Achievement badges even more.

"Very funny, guys. Seriously, you are going to love these. They are so luxurious, unlike anything we've ever produced in our EverAscend line. Victor really pulled out all the stops for Team VirtuPath. I can't wait for each of you to earn your own."

Grace continued, "The first badge is the EverDynamo. I love this design with the two hands clasping the glowing torch. It's such a great symbol of unity under pressure. The EverDynamo badge is earned when an individual goes

Ascending Vision

above and beyond to help the team succeed on a high-stakes project or deadline. It's all about relentless leadership!"

The team nodded their heads, waiting to hear about the second badge.

"I can already see some of you claiming that one. We definitely have strong contenders in this room. Here's the second one, the EverLume badge. This badge is earned by igniting innovation and contributing ideas that significantly enhance our team's performance and outcomes. What do you think about these?"

John paused and said with a sly grin, "I'll take EverLume for $1000, Alex. But seriously, you guys, remember that genius marketing campaign I pitched that nobody liked, but then it was a major hit? That's how we got that 32% marketing engagement increase."

"Well, John, don't forget who came up with the fashion show idea...that EverLume is mine, sir," Tori added playfully.

Brandon leaned in with confidence. "And Grace, did you say relentless leadership? See this empty space on my lovely VirtuPath shirt? The EverDynamo will find its home here by next week!"

"Brandon, just so we're clear, the EverDynamo badge comes with a strict rule: No caffeine IV drips allowed," Angela said with a laugh.

Grace enjoyed the team banter. "Loving this energy. You'll be earning these badges before you know it. Victor said 10 more Employee Achievement badges will be introduced within the next month, so stay tuned for even more goodness."

She touched the digital screenboard to reveal the second announcement. The screen read VAR in huge gold letters.

"Now for the second announcement. Here's a hint. V.A.R."

The team glanced at one another.

"Victor's Ambitious Rewards?" Brandon guessed.

"Victor's Absolute Rule? Also known as Victor's world domination plans?" Natasha quipped.

"No, I think it's Victor's All-Star Rewards," Angela added.

"Does anyone else find it hilarious that we all think the V stands for Victor?" Brandon asked with a laugh.

Grace rolled her eyes with a smile. "You guys are too much. I won't keep you in suspense any longer. We need to go to another part of the office for this one. Follow me." The entire team hopped up out of their seats, eager to see what this mysterious V.A.R. announcement was about.

Grace led the team over to the surprise in a nearby hallway. The entire wall was covered by a gold VirtuPath logo embossed curtain.

"Craig, I'll let you do the honors and pull back the curtain."

"Don't mind if I do, boss," Craig joked.

Craig pulled back the curtain to reveal an 8-foot tall by 12-foot wide digital display. A sleek sign above the display read "*Success Looks Like This.*"

Craig studied the display with curiosity. "What is this, Grace?"

"This is our brand new V.A.R. display—VirtuPath Augmented Reality. It's very cool. It's an interactive screen where you can preview how you look with the new Employee Achievement badges before you even receive them. There are company-wide badges and team-level badges already loaded up. You'll find EverDynamo and EverLume here so you can see how they look on you. Tori, come check it out first. I know it's going to trigger some fun social media ideas for you."

Tori was eager to see how the display worked. She found her name in the system and selected the EverLume from the menu. She marveled at her Augmented Reality reflection.

"Grace, you weren't kidding. These badges are next level. It is shimmering and I love the holographic elements in it. It almost looks alive. It screams opulence, and what's crazy is that this is only augmented reality. I can't wait to actually earn a real one and rock it proudly. Success DOES indeed look like this!"

Craig joked, "Tori, if that badge looks alive, don't let it start a TikTok account—next thing we know, it'll have more followers than we do."

Grace chuckled. "Ok, team. I knew you'd love this. I hate to be abrupt and break up the party, but we all need to get back to work, and I need to head over to Victor's office for my meeting. I'll be sure to let him know you all love the new badges. I'll leave out the whole world domination commentary. Have a great rest of your day and keep up the amazing work. You're all incredible."

Grace waved goodbye.

"*Victor's Ambitious Rewards.*" Grace murmured to herself as she walked toward his office. Brandon and the team had him figured out, but she wasn't sure that was a compliment.

What's on his mind today? I hope everything is ok. The day has started off so well, and I'd love to keep it that way.

CHAPTER 2

Fuels for Greatness

Grace knocked on Victor Graves' large dark wood office door. As she admired its intricate carvings, she imagined what it would feel like when the space was hers and she could freely walk right in.

"Grace, is that you?" Victor called out. "You're right on time. Come on in."

She opened the door and immediately noticed the significant changes that Victor had made to his space since she had been there two weeks earlier. In the office nook across from his oversized custom-designed desk was an elaborate display that reminded Grace of a shrine. She frowned slightly as she took it all in, the sheer scale of it bordering on overwhelming.

On the wall was a meticulously designed collection of framed photos of Victor celebrating a number of VirtuPath's milestone moments—Victor standing in front of the VirtuPath building on opening day, Victor giving an acceptance speech holding VirtuPath's first award in recognition of its excellence in the industry, Victor shaking hands with a group of celebrities on the day he signed a substantial contract to create custom awards for one of the branches of The Academy in Hollywood. A gold sign in the center of the photo collection read "Because Milestones Matter. Master the Moments."

In front of the wall was a glass case etched with the VirtuPath logo showcasing a number of badges that Grace had never seen before, mounted on red velvet. Some of the badges had what looked to be diamond accents. The dramatic lighting in the case gave the badges a stunning glow. She noticed a small engraved plaque as a centerpiece among the badges that read Victor Graves – The Original Dynamo.

Victor stood up behind his desk wearing a dark blue badge-covered blazer. Each unique badge was arranged symmetrically on both sides of the front, including the lapels, shoulders, and top half of the sleeves. The bottom of the sleeves had VirtuPath's motto embroidered: Always Forward. Always Virtu.

I want to mention the new office additions and some of the new badges on his blazer, but it's probably best to hear why he wanted to meet with me.

He gestured toward a chair in front of his desk. "Take a seat, Grace. We have some important things to discuss."

Grace sat in the center chair, excited and slightly nervous.

"So, how did the EverAscend team respond to the new Employee Achievement badges? These are total game-changers that will transform how our employees see themselves and the work that they do."

Grace leaned forward toward Victor. "The team is pretty pumped up about these badges, Victor. We were all impressed by how you managed to keep this project a secret from everyone. I showed them the EverDynamo and EverLume badges plus took them to see the VirtuPath Augmented Reality display. I think it's fair to say that they are eager to begin earning badges."

Victor smiled as he ran his finger over the platinum badge on this lapel.

"I knew they'd be excited. These Employee Achievement badges aren't mere awards or symbols. They are identities and fuels for greatness. When you wear one, you aren't solely celebrating your previous achievements; you are becoming the success you desire to be."

Victor paused for a moment, his gaze softening as he leaned back against his desk. "You know, Grace, this isn't just a project to me. It's a second chance." His voice dropped to a quieter, almost confessional tone. "I've been the guy who played it safe, who let fear hold him back. And I watched others surpass me, not because they were better but because they took risks I was too afraid to take. Never again."

Grace tilted her head, unsure how to respond. Victor's usual confidence felt muted, replaced by something raw and deeply personal.

"These Employee Achievement badges," he continued, holding up his lapel as if presenting evidence, "they're more than just recognition tools—they're proof that we can break free of limitations, real or imagined. That's why this has to work, Grace. For the team, for the company...for me."

Victor straightened, the flicker of vulnerability disappearing as quickly as it had surfaced. A faint smirk returned to his lips, and he shifted his weight, sitting on the edge of his desk with renewed composure.

His eyes locked on Grace's, his voice calm but edged with a sense of triumph. "And by the way, keeping this a secret was easy because I had a technology lab built in the old Apex conference room that we had closed off for the past year."

Grace tilted her head curiously. "A technology lab? Why did you need a technology lab for the badges?"

Victor laughed. "Can't get anything past you, Grace. Great question. That's what I was about to share with you. There's more to these Employee Achievement badges than I initially told you about. These badges are adaptive and embedded with technology that amplifies ambition."

"Amplify ambition? I'm not sure I understand what you mean, Victor."

Victor beamed with pride. "Grace, it's the future. The future of recognition. You'll learn more about that soon. In the meantime, let's get to the main reason I asked you to meet with me. I have a surprise for you."

The pride in Victor's eyes was unmistakable, but when he mentioned "amplifying ambition," his voice carried an edge that left her wondering. *Since when did ambition need amplifying?*

Victor walked to the back of his desk and opened a drawer. He pulled out a purple box with the VirtuPath logo embossed in gold on the cover. He walked over to Grace and slowly opened the box to reveal three shimmering badges. Grace held her breath. She recognized the EverLume badge right away, and the other two badges were beautiful yet unfamiliar.

"Victor, these are stunning!"

"Yes, they are, Grace. And they are yours. You have been a key player in VirtuPath's success, especially over the past two years that you've been the manager for the EverAscend team. Stand up; I want to present these to you properly."

Grace stood up, trying to find the proper balance of eagerness and calm.

Victor held up the first badge. "Grace, this is the VirtuVanguard badge. I had this one designed exclusively for the pioneers in the company. Vanguard is a group of people who are leading the way in new developments and ideas. You have surely earned it, as you've led the EverAscend team with courage and foresight."

He handed her the badge carefully. Grace smiled as she admired it, captivated by the soft glow that seemed to emanate from its surface. "You've earned it," Victor said with a nod of approval.

Grace placed the badge on the left side of her VirtuPath-branded Oxford shirt. She felt the slight pressure of the magnet beneath her shirt, grounding the badge in place.

Victor took the second badge out of the box and held it up with a knowing smile. "Look at the platinum accents on this beauty. You already know what this one is. It's the EverLume badge. It only makes sense that you would be the first to wear it. It's because of your creative genius that the VirtuPath Augmented Reality display came to life. I know it's going to be a hit with the entire company and be instrumental for our culture."

He gently placed the badge in Grace's hand. She carefully placed the badge next to the VirtuVanguard badge on her shirt, feeling another soft click as the magnet locked it into place. Was it just her imagination or was there a warm tingle where the magnet touched her skin? "Thank you so much, Victor," she said, her voice steady despite the lingering tingle.

"Save your gratitude for this last one, Grace. It's going to take your breath away."

Victor picked up the final badge from the velvet case. Grace was struck by the shifting colors in the crystal and the gold and platinum accents. Victor turned the badge around and placed it in Grace's hand. She read the inscription on the back that read *The EverGrace: Embody Success.*

"As you can see, this one was custom-designed for you. It's a limited edition, so limited that it only has one recipient. You. This EverGrace badge represents your ability to embody what VirtuPath stands for. This is about the potential I see in you. Keep up what you're doing, Grace, and someday, I may have to sell you the majority of this company and let you lead it."

Grace stumbled to put words together as she took the badge from Victor and placed it on the right side of her shirt. "I don't know what to say, Victor. I'm rarely speechless, but this is all so overwhelming. In a good way, of course. Victor, thank you."

As Grace walked out of Victor's office, a slight pulsing sensation emanated from the areas where each badge rested on her shirt.

Hmm...that's unusual. Maybe that's my ambition amplifying.

She laughed quietly to herself and headed back to her office. She still had some work to get done before heading out for lunch and an off-site client meeting.

Grace turned on her laptop and shuffled through her bag to find her favorite daily notebook. She opened her desk drawer to get a pen but paused as she noticed a small yellow paper with words written on it in familiar penmanship.

Here Elliott goes again.

Grace picked up the paper and read the note from Elliott Hart, a long-time Operations Director at VirtuPath and a consistent source of wise counsel.

Hi Grace,

Today marks another special milestone for you.

Call me when you can so we can celebrate and catch up on things.

Elliott

Grace smiled as she picked up the note. Elliott had a way of showing up at the right moments—quietly, without fanfare, yet always exactly when she needed it.

She remembered their first conversation seven years ago, two weeks into her job at VirtuPath. She had just left a meeting feeling overwhelmed by the company's relentless pace when Elliott found her staring blankly at the breakroom coffee machine. "It doesn't bite, you know," he'd said, his smile kind and reassuring. "It just spits out bad coffee." She had laughed despite herself, and somehow, that one small moment led to a conversation that grounded her—one about keeping her values intact in a place that often seemed focused on performance over everything else.

From that day forward, Elliott had become a steady presence in her life. He was the calm in her storm of ambition. When she doubted herself, he saw potential. When she was tempted to overwork herself into the ground, he pulled her back with questions like, *"Are you moving forward or just moving fast?"* Elliott was VirtuPath's Operations Director, but he never fully drank the Kool-Aid, as he liked to put it. "I'm here to focus on the roots, not just admire the blossoms," he'd once told her with a wink. Grace often wondered why he stayed, but she was glad he did.

Grace picked up her phone and dialed Elliott's number right away.

"You found my note, I see," Elliott said with a laugh in his voice.

"You always know how to get my attention, Elliott. Thank you for your kind words, as always. The badges are beautiful and receiving them was quite an honor today."

"You're welcome, Grace. I imagine Victor outdid himself in typical Victor Graves fashion. I look forward to hearing all the details."

Grace laughed, "Yes, he did. I am about to get some emails out, grab lunch, and then head to a client meeting. Are you free to have lunch tomorrow at 12:30?"

"Yes, that sounds like a plan, Grace. Enjoy the rest of your day, and I'll see you tomorrow."

Grace Under Pressure

Grace logged into her email account and addressed the high-priority items in her inbox. Finishing her work, she collected her bag and a few essentials for her client meeting and headed to the VirtuPath employee parking lot.

As she settled into the driver's seat, her hand drifted to the EverGrace badge. The contact sent a warm, prickling sensation crawling across her skin—subtle, but too strange to ignore.

CHAPTER 3

Obsession

Grace grabbed her coffee tumbler and slid her laptop bag over her shoulder. "Mia, I'm leaving in two minutes. Is Caleb ready?"

Mia, perched casually on the edge of the kitchen counter with her keys dangling in her hand, rolled her eyes. "He's brushing his teeth, like you didn't yell at him to do that 10 minutes ago."

"Let's not pretend you don't *also* need reminders, Miss Seventeen-and-Too-Cool-for-Mom," Grace replied with a smirk.

Caleb appeared at that moment, tugging on his backpack. "I'm ready; let's go." He paused mid-step, staring at the shimmering badges on Grace's shirt. "Mom...you're glowing. You look like you're collecting superhero power-ups."

"Super *mom* power-ups," Grace corrected with a grin. "And I need every one of them to help you move faster," she teased. "Mia, don't let him convince you to stop for donuts."

"Relax, Mom. I'm the responsible one, remember?" Mia grinned, already ushering Caleb toward the garage. "Come on, Caleb. The Badge Queen has places to be."

Grace Under Pressure

"Okay, Badge Queen, we're out!" Caleb called as he followed Mia into the garage.

Grace waved them off with a chuckle, appreciating how independent they'd become. Co-parenting had its challenges, but mornings like this—easy, lighthearted—reminded her that they were doing just fine.

Grace paused as she reached her car, catching her reflection in the side mirror. Her badges caught the light, gleaming as if they had a personality of their own. She shook her head with a small smile, opened the car door, and slid into the driver's seat. The familiar jasmine scent of the car wrapped around her as she tapped the dashboard, starting her favorite playlist. The soft rhythm of the music steadied her, nudging her into work mode.

Grace walked quickly through VirtuPath's front doors and immediately headed to the Summit Conference Room for her morning meeting with Team EverAscend. As she got closer to the conference room, she could already hear the team's conversation and laughter. She lowered her eyes at the glistening badges on her shirt. *Sounds like the coffee has already kicked in this morning.* They were going to go nuts when they saw these badges. She mentally braced herself to redirect their focus or risk the meeting turning into a circus.

She reviewed the agenda in her mind as she entered the room. The aroma of fresh coffee lingered in the air, but as

Obsession

soon as Grace stepped inside, the volume in the room quieted. The team's eyes immediately locked on her badges.

Tori was the first to speak up. "Graaaaaace, look at you! Three badges in less than 24 hours?!?"

Brandon took a sip of his coffee. "Natasha, we might need to revisit that Java Champion badge design and add some platinum accents because Grace has gone Next Level on us! Those aren't EverAscend; those must be EverElite!"

Natasha laughed in agreement. "That's for sure."

Angela, unable to resist, chimed in as she sat next to Brandon. "Brandon, focus. We need to get a super innovative sales strategy together so we can earn some badges with a quickness. I passed the V.A.R. display three times today already, and I must say that I look *real good* sportin' the EverLume."

"Okay, team, simmer down," Grace said lightly, shaking off the moment. "Yes, the badges are awesome, but let's focus on delighting our customers more than ourselves right now. Today we're diving into product development and the next steps for our marketing campaign. Craig, are you ready?"

Craig stood quickly and walked to the head of the table. "Absolutely! I've been working my tail off getting this presentation ready, and I can't wait for the team's feedback. Brandon, hit the button for me, please."

"You got it." Brandon pressed the button, and the digital screen emerged, glowing softly as it reflected off the sleek table. He got up to pour himself another cup of coffee as Craig started his presentation.

"Ladies and gentlemen of Team EverAscend," Craig began with dramatic flair, "I introduce to you our newest product line: the EverAscend Wearables!" He touched the display, revealing three designs.

"This is a great time," Craig continued, "to help people celebrate and showcase their achievements in new ways with Wearables. Here are the initial mock-ups for a bracelet, pendant, and arm cuff. All of them incorporate one of our EverAscend badges. I need your feedback. Should we integrate only one badge within the design, or should we design each of the Wearables to be interchangeable for those who may have more than one of our badges?"

Grace watched as Craig awaited a flurry of feedback from the team.

Hmmm...the team really seems distracted. I better help Craig out.

"Craig, I'm loving these designs," Grace said, trying to ground the conversation and redirect the room's energy. "I have some thoughts, but let's hear what the team thinks first."

Brandon raised a hand, half-grinning. "Just wondering—are these going to feature the new Employee Achievement badges? Asking for a friend...by which I mean *me*."

Angela chimed in, "Okay, I'm with Brandon—the EverLume badge would look *amazing* as a pendant. Grace, seriously, you're making the rest of us look bad!"

Tori leaned forward, her nails tapping rhythmically against her phone as she scrolled. "I'm kinda partial to the bracelet. You know what would be cool for our IG page? If we took a team photo with just our arms showing off our bracelets. The caption could be 'EverAscending, one wrist at a time!' or maybe 'The Ultimate Badge Flex – who wore it best? Hashtag Badge Goals!' What do you guys think?"

"Guys," Grace said, her voice a little firmer. "Let's focus on Craig's question about the design. What do you think—one badge per piece or interchangeable?"

The team responded in agreement for interchangeable designs, but Grace couldn't shake the feeling that they weren't truly listening.

Craig sighed in relief, clearly sensing the same distraction. "Thanks, everyone. Now let's do a quick poll on names: AscendWear, VirtuWear, or VirtuEdge."

Tori perked up, finally looking away from her phone. "Team VirtuEdge all the way! The tagline could be 'VirtuEdge: Elevate Every Moment.'"

Angela added with a smirk, "AscendWear sounds like mountain climber gear. VirtuWear makes me think of yoga pants."

Brandon shrugged sheepishly. "Why isn't EverWear one of the options? Boom. Easy peasy."

Natasha, scribbling in her notebook filled with sketches, paused and glanced up with a smirk. "Guys, pick whatever you want. I'm working on a design concept proposal for our Employee Achievement badges. Grace's blinged-out shirt is distracting...oh, I mean inspiring...me!"

Something in Grace's chest tightened. *What's with them today? They're obsessed.*

"Craig, thank you," Grace said, clearing her throat. "Sounds like we've agreed on interchangeable designs. As for the naming decision, I'll leave that to John and the marketing team to finalize. Send it to me for approval next week."

She looked to the rest of the team. "Team, I know it's a little bit early, but let's go ahead and end today's meeting. We'll save the marketing campaign discussion for tomorrow, and then we'll do the metrics review. See you tomorrow morning. Enjoy your day."

The team nodded, but Grace saw it—the small flickers of disappointment that the discussion was over. She gathered her tablet and notebook, forcing a smile. As she exited the conference room, her mind refused to quiet. *Are these badges really fueling greatness, or are they becoming something else entirely?*

Grace slipped into her office and dropped her things onto the desk, sinking into her chair. Her hand instinctively found the EverGrace badge. This time, the weight felt heavier and the heat against her skin undeniable. She opened her drawer and picked up Elliott's note from the day before, reading it again. *"Another special milestone for you."*

Yesterday, those words had sounded celebratory. Today, they felt like a nudge—an invitation to explore more of what was swirling around in her mind and heart. The team's distracted energy. The warmth and tingling from the badges. Victor's talk of "amplifying ambition."

What am I missing? Reaching for her phone, she dialed Elliott.

"Elliott, I know we have plans for lunch already, but can we meet earlier and do brunch?"

CHAPTER 4

Whispers of Truth

Grace pulled into the parking lot of The Willow Grove Café, relieved that Elliott had adjusted his schedule for an earlier brunch. The weather was beautiful—sunny with a slight breeze—the ideal atmosphere for outdoor dining.

She stepped into the café. The hostess warmly greeted her and escorted her to the patio, where she settled her at a small table for two overlooking the garden. Grace enjoyed the faint aroma of warm pastries coming from the open doors of the café and the stillness of the patio. It was the perfect refuge after the chaos of her morning. She needed to calm the storm that had been brewing in her mind since leaving the team meeting.

Grace smiled as she saw Elliott enter the patio area. He was carrying a worn, brown journal, as he often did when they met. She stood up to give him a hug, one that she desperately needed. "Elliott, it's so good to see you. Thank you for shifting your schedule today. It means so much to me."

"Of course, Grace. I've been looking forward to this. Though I must say, I almost didn't see you with all of that sparkling light coming off all of those badges," Elliott joked, sliding into the rustic chair.

"Oh, Elliott, if I have to hear one more comment about these badges today…" Grace said, her voice tinged with exasperation.

The server came to the table to take their coffee and entrée orders. As he left, Elliott leaned toward Grace, a knowing look in his eyes. "So, Grace, let's talk. You clearly have a lot on your mind. What's going on up in there?" he asked, gesturing lightly toward her head.

"You're right, Elliott. It's been a bit of an emotional whirlwind over the past two days. I've been reflecting, and while my thoughts are still taking shape, I think I've boiled them down to two main concerns."

Grace took a deep breath and continued, "Number one, I'm concerned about Team EverAscend and the impact these new Employee Achievement badges have on them. I'm torn because they are motivating and stunningly beautiful, but they could also undermine the meaningful collaboration we need to serve our customers well. Number two, and I don't know exactly how to say this, but I'm struggling with discerning Victor's motives—with VirtuPath overall and with me personally. I love my team, I love the mission of this company, and I want to continue to grow in leadership here. I'm optimistic, yet I'm uneasy. Do I sound like a lunatic?"

Elliott gave a soft, reassuring smile. "No, Grace, you don't sound like a lunatic at all. You've reached a milestone—one you should celebrate because you've earned it. But milestones also come with growing pains. This isn't really about the badges; this is an opportunity to increase your leadership capacity. Take a step back and look at the bigger picture. What might this moment be preparing you for?"

Grace's shoulders relaxed slightly. "Thank you, Elliott. That's solid advice, and I'll think more about that. But can we talk about something Victor said that is really bugging me? He said the Employee Achievement badges weren't mere awards or symbols. They are identities and fuels for greatness. He also mentioned that they are tech-enabled to amplify ambition. Got any sage wisdom on all of that?" she asked with a laugh.

The server arrived and placed Grace's garden omelet and Elliott's lemon ricotta pancakes on the table before them. He left briefly and returned with two steaming coffee mugs.

"Wow, thank you. These pancakes look amazing!" Elliott said with enthusiasm, giving the server a grateful nod as he turned and headed back into the café. He took a bite of his pancakes and continued, "Amplify ambition? Hmm....that's not just technology; it's psychology, even neuroscience. Do you know what's actually embedded in those badges?"

"No, that's the thing," Grace admitted. "Victor was vague, but he seemed so sure of their potential."

Elliott leaned back, his brow furrowed. "Victor's excitement makes sense when you know where he's coming from. Before VirtuPath, he ran an event production company. It was supposed to be his big break, but one bad deal and everything fell apart. He lost the business, his finances, and almost his reputation. When VirtuPath took off, it wasn't just about building a company—it was about proving he could do the impossible, that he could rise from the ashes."

Grace frowned, stirring her coffee. "So, these badges are part of that?"

"In a way," Elliott said. "To Victor, they're more than just tools—they're his legacy. But ambition like his... it can blur the lines. When you're driven by the need to prove yourself, you sometimes stop asking if you should and focus only on if you can."

Grace let his words settle, her mind swirling with questions. Was this about redemption? Or control? She pushed her omelet around the plate absentmindedly, her appetite waning. Elliott noticed and smiled gently.

"Grace, you're gifted with the ability to see what others often don't. Keep observing. You'll find the answers you're looking for. And remember—you're not alone. I'm here with you every step of the way."

"Thank you, Elliott," Grace said, forcing a smile. "I don't know what I'd do without your wisdom."

"Well," Elliott said, dabbing at his mouth with his napkin, "I'm just a sounding board. You already know what you need to do—you just need space to hear it clearly."

Grace nodded, his words resonating. As the server came by to clear their plates, Elliott gestured to Grace's half-eaten omelet. "Done with this?" he asked.

"Yes, thanks," Grace said, standing as she slipped her bag over her shoulder. She glanced toward the park next door, the sight of the willows swaying in the breeze pulling her attention. "I think I'm going to take your advice and give myself that space. I'll head over to the park for a little while before heading back to the office."

Elliott rose and gave her a hug. "Good. That's exactly what you need. I'll take care of the bill—go decompress. And Grace?" He caught her gaze, his voice soft but resolute. "You're not alone. See you soon."

She gave him a grateful smile and stepped toward the garden path that led to the park. She savored the crisp breeze and the scent of blooming flowers along the pathway. By the time she reached the pond, she spotted a weathered bench in the shade of a willow tree. The birds chirping nearby and the stillness of the water captured her. She settled onto the bench and released a sigh.

I'm increasing my leadership capacity. I have what it takes to navigate this. I can trust my intuition, she thought to herself as she pondered her conversation with Elliott.

She mentally replayed Victor's statements: *"These badges aren't mere awards or symbols. They are identities and fuels for greatness."* While Grace wrestled with determining the motive behind those words, her thoughts were interrupted by a strong simultaneous tingling—almost electric—sensation from the VirtuVanguard and EverLume badges on the left side of her shirt.

Grace lightly touched her EverGrace badge and was startled by the intense pulse that seemed to be emanating from it. She ignored it and went back to replaying Victor's statements, but the sensation persisted. She stood up from the bench and began to pace around the park. As she walked, a thought came to her—sharp and sudden, almost like an intrusion. It was something Elliott said to her many times before, his words now breaking through the noise of her mind with quiet clarity.

Sometimes you have to let go of the good to grab hold of the great. She repeated Elliott's words to herself, the truth of them settling in her heart, but with the uncertainty of what they meant for her in this moment. She continued to reflect as she walked back toward her car. *Ambition amplified. But at what cost? And if these badges amplify ambition, what happens when they're gone?*

Grace's hand hovered over the EverGrace badge, which was even warmer than it was earlier at the office. "Not yet," she whispered as she allowed her hand to drop to her side. The decision would wait—tomorrow held its own clarity.

CHAPTER 5

Fractured Ambition

Grace's alarm buzzed at 6:30 a.m. She groaned softly, reaching to silence it, and lay still for a moment, staring at the ceiling as yesterday's events replayed in her mind.

"Moooom! Did you move my sneakers again?" Caleb's voice rang out from the hallway, breaking through her thoughts.

"No, Caleb! Check under the couch," Grace called back, dragging herself upright. She rubbed her temples, already bracing for the whirlwind of the morning. The tension in her chest lingered as she headed for the bathroom, the thought of the badges pulsing faintly in the back of her mind.

The warmth of a long shower did little to ease the tension she was feeling. Wrapping herself in a towel, she walked into her closet. She slipped into her undergarments and pants, then grabbed a neatly pressed purple Oxford shirt from the hanger. She reached for the badges on her dresser and attached each badge in its usual place.

By the time Grace emerged, dressed and still uneasy, Caleb was clambering around the living room, a single sneaker in hand, while Mia sipped on a smoothie at the kitchen counter.

"Found them," Caleb announced, holding up the missing shoe with exaggerated triumph.

Mia glanced over at Grace and raised an eyebrow. "You're wearing those badges again? Thought you said they felt like a distraction last night." She paused, her tone light but pointed. "Everything okay, Mom?"

"I'm fine," Grace said quickly. "Now, you two, out the door before you're late. Don't make me text your dad about tardy records again."

Caleb groaned dramatically as he slung his backpack over his shoulder. "Relax, Badge Queen, we're going! Come on, Mia."

Mia rolled her eyes but smiled as she grabbed her keys. "We'll see you tonight, Mom. Don't let those badges steal your soul or anything."

Grace laughed faintly as they left, the door clicking shut behind them. She stepped in front of the hallway mirror. Her reflection stared back, calm on the surface but unsettled in her gut. Her gaze drifted to the badges on her shirt, the EverGrace badge subtly pulsing against her chest.

Something isn't right with these badges. Today is a good day not to wear them. The team meeting will probably be way more productive without the distraction anyway.

She reached up and began to remove the VirtuVanguard badge. As she pulled, the magnet resisted, clinging to her skin with an unsettling grip. The moment the badge detached from her shirt, a sharp, searing pain tore through her chest and radiated up through her shoulder. She gasped, her eyes widening in horror as she looked down. Beneath the spot where the badge had rested, a raw, open wound glistened against her skin, blood pooling faintly around the edges. Her hand trembled as panic set in. Instinctively, she put the badge back into place and the wound vanished, leaving no trace of its existence.

"What is happening to me?!?" she exclaimed, her eyes wide and voice cracking with panic. Her mind raced. She remembered how lifeless the badges always were when she wasn't wearing them. But attached to her, they pulsed with an eerie vitality.

"They're not just badges," she whispered, Victor's words echoing in her mind. "They're identities. Fuels for greatness. They're adaptive. They amplify ambition."

She took a breath, her eyes still locked on the mirror.

I have to get to the bottom of this. And I need to talk to Elliott.

Arriving at the VirtuPath offices, she made her way to the conference room a half hour early, hoping to pull herself together before the usual pre-meeting coffee brewing and morning banter began. She forced herself to act as normal as possible. She needed time to process and plan her next steps.

She dropped into the chair at the head of the table and pulled out her phone. Quickly, she typed out a text to Elliott: *Can we talk? Urgent. Let me know when you're free.*

With a sigh, she placed her phone on the table and closed her eyes, pressing her fingertips to her temples. *Breathe, Grace. Just act normal. Marketing campaigns. Metrics. That's the agenda. You can do this. You have to do this.*

The ache in her shoulder had eased, but her mind was still occupied with the morning's events. She practiced one of the breathing techniques Elliott had taught her years ago, counting to five with each inhale and exhale, trying to anchor herself.

A few minutes passed, and the sound of footsteps and lighthearted chatter in the hallway broke through her moment of stillness.

The team is here. Marketing campaigns. Metrics. Focus, Grace. You've got this.

"Good morning, Madam Rock Star!" John's voice boomed as he entered the room, grinning at Grace. Behind him, Brandon and Angela followed, their conversation already in full swing.

"Angela, I'm telling you, we could pull off a Badge of the Month subscription model for our corporate clients, reinforcing all the goodness that comes from celebration and recognition."

"Maybe, Brandon," Angela countered, smirking, "but I think customization is where the real money is at. Both our corporate and retail customers have been asking for it for years. If we lean into that, we could easily 2x, maybe even 3x, our lifetime customer value."

Grace straightened in her chair, relief washing over her as she overheard their conversation. For once, they weren't obsessing over the Employee Achievement badges. *Good. Let's keep it this way.*

"Good morning, team," Grace said, her voice sounding steadier than she felt. "Grab your coffee and we'll start in a moment."

The rest of the team trickled in, snacks and mugs in hand, as they settled into their usual seats around the table. Grace took a deep breath as John walked to the head of the table, activating the digital screen with a quick touch. The display illuminated with vibrant graphics and marketing campaign visuals for the EverAscend badges.

John launched into his presentation with his usual flair. "...And that's where we see the opportunity for increased brand engagement," John concluded, pointing to a chart that illustrated promising growth projections. "It's all about leveraging our storytelling strategy to connect customers' accomplishments with something tangible and memorable. By positioning the badges as essential for recognizing top performance, we can turn EverAscend into more than a product for our customers—it's a culture."

Brandon nodded enthusiastically. "Absolutely. These badges are game-changers—for them and for us. We should stockpile a set just for Team EverAscend."

Grace smiled softly, but her focus was elsewhere. *Stay focused, Grace. Metrics are next. Be present.*

Angela transitioned the conversation seamlessly. "This has been a strong sales week, everyone—actually, a strong month. Brandon and I are finalizing updates to our sales strategy for next quarter, which should keep this momentum going."

The team chimed in with affirmations and questions, but Grace found her attention slipping. Her thoughts drifted to Elliott's possible response to her text. She glanced at her phone, tempted to check for a message, but Brandon leaned over and nudged her shoulder playfully. "So, Grace, when do we get to earn our own badges? Team EverAscend is carrying this whole company on our shoulders!"

Angela chimed in, laughing. "Yeah, Grace, spill the beans. Are we talking next week, next month? What do we have to do to get them sooner?"

The entire team was smiling inquisitively at Grace, anticipating her response.

They are so eager and motivated. I can't alarm them right now. They will have more questions than I have answers.

"I believe we're getting close. I have a meeting with Victor next week and will be able to give you a definitive answer. Keep up the amazing work, team. You'll have those badges stacked in no time," Grace said, mustering as much positive energy as possible.

The team nodded, and the discussion returned to the remaining metrics review. After the final presentation, the team disbanded, and Grace walked to her office. She sat at her desk and checked her phone for a message from Elliott. Relieved, she read the message that had come through during the team meeting: Always have time for you. Meet me at the café when your team meeting ends. I'll be there waiting.

What a Godsend. Although I don't know if he's ready for this wild turn of events.

Grace grabbed her belongings and left her office. As she walked through the VirtuPath halls, all her badges began to pulse erratically, so intense they seemed to echo through her thin frame. Her vision blurred, causing her to stagger and grip the wall for support. The EverGrace badge was hot against her skin as if trying to fuse with her body.

This is bad. Really bad.

She managed to get to her car in the parking lot and collapsed into the driver's seat, fear gripping her in a way that was unfamiliar.

She whispered to herself, "I need to get to Elliott and figure this out...and fast."

CHAPTER 6

Burning Questions

Grace drove to The Willow Grove Café, battling her thoughts and physical pain at once. The burning sensation from the EverGrace badge was unrelenting, and she wondered how long it was going to last and if it was going to get any worse.

Is this an accidental technical defect? Or is it some sort of sadistic plot? Why would Victor want to harm me or any of the VirtuPath employees intentionally? She contemplated the possibilities with angst.

When Grace arrived in the parking lot, the burning sensation eased, but the discomfort in her chest and shoulder remained. She took a few deep breaths, opened her car door, and headed toward the café.

Elliott, noticing the distress on Grace's face, gave her a hug and ushered her to their usual spot on the patio with the garden view. Two glasses of water and a stainless steel kettle with two tea cups were on the table; an assortment of teas and a small honey container were beside them. Elliott explained as he pulled out a chair for Grace to sit, "I took the liberty to order a few essentials for us before you arrived."

"Thank you, Elliott, I appreciate it." She paused, unsure of what to say next.

Grace Under Pressure

Elliott pressed gently, "Grace, talk to me. What happened this morning?"

Grace hesitated, her fingers tightening around the warm cup. "Elliott, I'm not even sure how to explain this. The badges... they're not what they seem. This morning, I tried to take one off—just one—and the pain was immediate, sharp, like... like something vital was being ripped away. When I looked down, there was a deep wound, and then when I quickly put the badge back on, it vanished. I don't know, Elliott. It's like the badges are a part of me now, somehow."

She paused, her eyes searching Elliott's face for a reaction. "I know this sounds weird, but they feel... alive. When they're on me, they pulse, almost like they have a heartbeat. They get uncomfortable and hot, dangerously hot, at times. It's really scary. And I don't know what to think about Victor right now. Is this intentional? Is it an accident? What do I do now, and how do I protect my team? They are excited about earning their Employee Achievement badges, and I'm unsure whether they will be safe."

Elliott leaned forward. "Grace, I'm so sorry you're dealing with this. That sounds painful in more ways than one. Here's the truth though. You're stronger than you feel right now...and this challenge? Look at it as a test. I'll walk with you through it, but you need to decide: will this break you or refine you?"

Grace's chin dipped slightly. "Elliott, I hear what you are saying, but I feel like everything is spiraling out of my control. The badges, Victor, my team...it's like I am losing my grip."

"Control. It's a comforting lie. The truth is that you are not losing control because you cannot lose what you never had."

Grace chuckled a little. "Let me get you a microphone so you can drop it." Her expression turned serious, "I can't control everything, Elliott, but I can't just sit here and do nothing."

"What you need is a change in focus. Start by asking yourself: What's the next small step you can take to move forward, not out of fear, but with clarity and purpose?" Elliott offered.

Grace exhaled, her grip on the cup relaxing slightly. "I don't even know where to start."

Elliott smiled. "Sometimes, the starting point isn't something you do—it's something you hear or sense. Grace, you've been good at listening to others as long as I've known you, but right now, you need to listen deeply. Not just to the noise around you or even to your fears, but to the quiet whispers—the ones that come when you're still enough to hear them."

He paused, letting his words sink in before continuing. "The answers are there, Grace. They always were. They always are. They always will be."

"And what if I don't find the answers fast enough, Elliott?"

"You will. But not by rushing." Elliott paused. "Remember, your strength doesn't come from knowing everything—it comes from trusting what you're being shown, one step at a time. Quiet your fears, and listen. The rest will follow."

Grace took a final sip of her chai tea and thanked Elliott for his support. She stepped out of the café, her thoughts swirling. She adjusted the strap of her purse, her hand brushing against the EverGrace badge. The memory of its pulsing heat made her wince. *How did something meant to celebrate success turn into... this?* The question lingered, heavy and unanswered.

She exhaled slowly. *My team is depending on me. If I can't get to the bottom of this, how long before these badges start affecting them, too? This isn't just about me. It's about something bigger. And when the time comes, I'll face it head-on.*

CHAPTER 7

Wings of Stillness

Grace arrived at VirtuPath Monday morning, her body drained from a restless weekend. The purple "Always Forward. Always Virtu." sign didn't inspire her as it used to. As she walked through the hallway, the faint pulses of her badges pressed against her awareness, a constant and unsettling reminder. Her body still ached from Friday's attempted removal.

Her mind drifted to the chaos of the weekend at home. Caleb's science project had exploded, leaving a baking soda volcano mess on the kitchen counter. Mia, frustrated with applying for college scholarships, had needed help formatting her essays. Balancing parenting, work, and her mounting unease felt like juggling with one hand tied behind her back.

Even as she stood in the pristine VirtuPath hallways, Grace could still hear Caleb's triumphant laugh when they finally got the volcano to work and Mia's sweet "Thanks, Mom," after she stayed up late reviewing her essay. Those moments anchored her—but today, even the thought of them couldn't shake the weight in her chest.

"Rise and Grind! Ready for another big week?" a colleague called as she hurried past, not waiting for Grace's response. She sighed, relieved that she didn't need to answer, and headed to the conference room to prepare for the Team EverAscend meeting. She prepared a cup of coffee and gathered her thoughts before the team arrived.

The team trickled into the conference room, energized from the weekend. Brandon boasted, "I scored a new client this weekend! I didn't want to risk losing the deal, so I went back and forth between phone and email with their Human Resources Director on Saturday. Their first order for $10,000 worth of products was submitted first thing this morning. Let me grab my celebratory cup of coffee right now."

Angela smiled with a wink. "Great work, Brandon!"

Grace grinned. "Congratulations on another happy customer, Brandon!" She turned to the rest of the team. "Okay, team, let's get started. It's the final week of the month, and we have plenty to cover. We'll start with updates and then move into our Monday Marketing discussion."

The team settled into their usual seats.

"First, I know you all have been eager to hear more about the Employee Achievement badges. Let me go ahead and get that out of the way so we can focus for the rest of the meeting," Grace said with a light chuckle. "My meeting with Victor is tomorrow, so I'll have some more updates for you then."

Angela chimed in, "I think Team EverAscend has been crushing it lately, Grace! It's time we see our sexy new badges, not just virtually on that V.A.R. display, but physically on us."

"Plus I have reel ideas for our social profiles that will showcase the team's badges and encourage our clients to celebrate their employees more. It will be fun and boost sales. I worked on a campaign plan for it late last night. So you see...this isn't just about us getting to sport sexy new badges." Tori added.

"But it also is," Angela quickly retorted with a smile.

The team laughed and then settled down to await Grace's instructions or additional updates.

A faint tension settled in Grace's chest as Brandon and Angela's casual comments about working late and on weekends echoed in her mind. Forcing a smile, she responded. "Well, in that case, I guess we better get you guys some badges. Do any of you have any key updates to add before we begin the Marketing Monday discussion?"

Grace nodded along as each team member provided their update, though their words seemed to blur together. Her focus wavered, and the ache in her chest deepened.

As the team transitioned into the marketing discussion, John stood and activated the sleek digital screen at the head of the table. "Okay, team," John began energetically, "first I need to say, Tori, your content strategies are killing it—our post likes and shares are at an all-time high."

"Thanks, John!" Tori said with a grin. "Wait until you see the short-form videos I have lined up for YouTube next month."

John continued, "If we boost excitement with some of our soon-to-be-released products and personalization options in our marketing, I think we can drive even more engagement and sales. Craig, I'm not sure how far along we are with the Wearables. Angela, Brandon—you probably have thoughts on personalization?"

Grace's badges heated up, the faint pulsing turning sharper, more insistent. She shifted in her chair, but the discomfort pressed harder. The words around her were blurred, and a bead of sweat slid down her temple.

"Grace, what do you think?"

John's voice caught her attention. She stammered in her response, "Oh, umm...yes, it sounds like you all are on the right track. Keep refining those ideas, and let's just make sure the final plan aligns with our broader goals."

Her badges pulsed again, and the heat from the EverGrace badge was almost unbearable. She reached for her water bottle and took a sip, her focus blurred as she did her best to hide her discomfort from the team. "Let's wrap up the meeting here," Grace said, standing to signal the end.

"Thank you everyone. I'll follow up with updates later this week."

The team filed out of the conference room, exchanging energetic chatter, and Grace lingered behind to avoid any further direct interaction.

I hate lying to the team like this. The team deserves badges, but what if they are hurt by them? I have to confront Victor about this before it's too late. But how?

Grace left the conference room to head back to her office.

"Hey Grace, you gotta sec?" Angela asked as she jogged toward her.

Grace nodded.

"Grace, you've been carrying the weight of EverAscend on your back, and you need a break—like, a real one. Why don't you leave the office and take a mental health day or something? We can hold things down here." Angela placed her hand lightly on Grace's shoulder and walked away.

Grace watched Angela walk away, her words lingering. A mental health day—could that really change anything? It seemed superficial, like patching a wound that needed surgery. Still, maybe Angela was onto something—just not in the way she imagined.

Grace drove over to the park next to The Willow Grove Café. She found a bench in a quiet, shaded area next to a walking path and sat down. Her phone vibrated, and as she unlocked her phone to review her notification alerts, she found herself mindlessly scrolling through her social media newsfeed. Her EverGrace badge pulsed faintly, reminding her that avoidance is not the answer. Grace put her phone back into her purse and took a deep breath. She closed her eyes and recalled Elliott's words from their last meeting:

"Right now, you need to listen deeply. Not just to the noise around you or even to your fears, but to the quiet whispers—the ones that come when you're still enough to hear them."

Maybe she needed to quiet her soul so she could hear and confront what she'd been avoiding. As she sat quietly, time seemed to stand still. Suddenly, a sense of panic swept over Grace.

What if I hear something I'm not ready to face? What if rest means letting go of everything I've built here?

She wanted clarity but dreaded its price. The EverGrace badge hummed faintly, its heat seeping through her shirt. It wasn't painful, but its energy carried an accusatory weight, as if mocking her avoidance. Her hands gripped the bench, her breath quick and uneven as the badge pulsed relentlessly against her chest.

A white-winged dove cooed nearby, catching Grace's attention. It perched on a branch, head tilted, its eyes briefly locking with hers. She watched as the dove took flight and effortlessly glided through the trees. She exhaled slowly. Maybe stillness wasn't holding her back—maybe it was setting her free. She took another deep breath, dropped her shoulders, and released her frantic thoughts as the tension eased in her body. The EverGrace badge cooled slightly. With her mind quieted, a memory resurfaced from a previous conversation with Victor. *"When you wear one, you aren't solely celebrating your previous achievements; you are becoming the success you desire to be."*

The words replayed in her mind, cutting with new meaning, like a blade slicing through the fog of her doubts. *These Employee Achievement badges weren't created to celebrate us—they were designed to control us.*

Grace's stomach churned. Had he known all along? She opened her eyes, feeling a small yet significant sense of clarity. She didn't have all the answers yet, but she had clarity where it mattered most: tomorrow, she would face Victor—and confront the reality waiting beneath the surface.

CHAPTER 8

Beneath the Surface

Grace woke up restless. The clarity she'd gained at the park brought a clash of emotions—strength on one side, anxiety on the other, each pulling her in opposite directions. As she showered and dressed, her thoughts circled around the upcoming meeting with Victor. What would she say? How would she say it? How would he react? Possible openings played out in her mind:

Victor, can we talk more about the badge technology?

Victor, I think there may be a problem with the Employee Achievement badges.

Hey Victor, I need to tell you something I've been experiencing with my badges.

Each scenario carried an air of uncertainty, but Grace knew she couldn't let her nerves take control. Her resolve strengthened as she stood before the mirror, adjusting her EverGrace badge. *I'll find the right words when the time comes,* she told herself. She'd rescheduled the Team EverAscend meeting for the afternoon since Victor was only available in the morning. The timing worked in her favor; she could share updates with the team about the much-anticipated badges once she'd spoken to Victor. But even as she tried to frame the change as practical, the thought of the

Grace Under Pressure

team's excitement about the badges still added to the pressure. She wasn't certain that any update she could give today would be a good one.

She arrived at VirtuPath, and after dropping off her bags in her office, she headed to meet with Victor. As she approached his office door, it opened abruptly and Victor walked out. "Good morning, Grace. Instead of meeting in my office, let's head over to the technology lab. I think it will help put everything into perspective."

His words caught her off guard. *Why the lab?* For a moment, a glimmer of hope arose. *Does he really not see the harm these badges could cause—or is he deliberately avoiding it? Maybe I can get some answers without sounding the alarm.* "Sure, Victor, that sounds great."

Victor set a brisk pace as they moved through VirtuPath's hallways. Grace followed, the pulse of her badges a reminder of the stakes ahead. Victor glanced back briefly with his usual confident smile and motioned toward an unmarked door at the end of the hall. *Stay composed, Grace. This isn't just about badges; this is about finding the truth.*

As they continued toward the lab, Grace inquired, "Victor, what inspired the concept of amplifying ambition through technology? It seems like such a unique approach."

"It's part of the bigger groundbreaking picture, Grace. I'm calling it *VirtuPath Vision 360: The Future of Work.* It's going to redefine workplace culture, and you and your team are right at the center of it all. Exciting times are ahead for all of us...." Victor paused, looking directly at Grace, his voice softening slightly as he added, "...if you choose to lead your team how I know you can."

Grace instinctively wanted to react but reminded herself of Elliott's advice to listen deeply and let answers emerge. She nodded instead.

Victor opened the door to the lab, and Grace was shocked at what she saw. Months ago, it was a standard conference room, and now she was staring at a high-tech environment filled with monitors and humming machines. Victor gestured proudly to the setup. "Welcome to the engine of VirtuPath's future. I've been waiting for the right time to show you this, Grace. You're about to see the heartbeat of our next evolution—the tools that will not only transform VirtuPath but redefine performance and recognition on a global scale."

He led her to one of the machines, where several prototypes were displayed. "This is *AscendGlobal,* the pilot program that will launch our *VirtuPath Vision 360* initiative. The program includes premium Employee Achievement badges, gamified Wearables, and Digital Recognition Boards that publicly celebrate achievements in real time. Here's the thing, Grace. We have to eat our own cooking first, so the pilot program begins right here at VirtuPath. The new tech-enabled badges? EverAscend 2.0. It starts with us, then moves into the broader corporate community."

Grace struggled to maintain her composure as Victor's words sunk in. *This isn't just about my team or even this company. If this tech goes live on a global scale, how many lives will be manipulated, how many people will physically suffer before anyone realizes what's happening?* The room seemed colder now, the hum of the machines more ominous. *Whether Victor doesn't see the danger, or worse, if he does and doesn't care…either way, this is a ticking time bomb, and I'm holding the match.*

Victor led Grace over to one of the prototyping machines. "You wanted to understand more about the technology? Here's where the magic happens. These microchips amplify ambition, empowering employees without the added pressure. When we started, I didn't realize how far we could push performance—but now? We've reached cutting-edge alignment between ambition and achievement."

Grace's doubts deepened at his lack of transparency.

Victor's enthusiasm quickly shifted to a serious tone as he gave Grace that same intense look he'd given her before entering the lab. "Grace, it's been a week since you've had your own Employee Achievement badges, and I've yet to see you roll them out to your team. AscendSummit, our major industry press event, is coming up, and we have to get some early wins to share. You're typically such a quick mover." Victor tilted his head with a slight chuckle, "I'm wondering if the EverGrace badge has a defect or something."

This is a good time to say something. Grace hesitated. "Victor, I appreciate the innovation behind this, truly. But I've noticed something unusual about the badges since I started wearing them. They feel...intrusive. It's almost as if they... adapt to me, to my emotions. Is that intentional?" She tried to keep her tone neutral, but her hands tightened at her sides.

Victor raised an eyebrow and smiled, his tone calm and reassuring. "Adapting to the wearer is exactly the point. These badges are designed to meet each individual where they are and take them further. It's not intrusive, Grace; it's empowering. It's about helping people rise to the occasion without the usual barriers."

The machine's screen suddenly flickered, displaying the words "J. Cain Initiative—Phase 2." Adrenaline surged through Grace, her pulse quickening. She opened her mouth to ask, but Victor tapped a button, closing the window with a casual chuckle. "Oops, wrong file," he said lightly.

Grace hesitated, her voice measured as she asked, "What's the J. Cain Initiative?"

Victor straightened, giving her his usual confident smile, but there was a flicker of something else—annoyance? Deflection? "Just an internal project that's still in development—Grace, there's no need to overanalyze here. Every great innovation feels strange at first. You've been around long enough to know that. Don't let discomfort cloud your vision."

Grace nodded slowly, his easy dismissal deepening her unease. Whatever the J. Cain Initiative was, she doubted it was "nothing."

Victor grabbed a medium-sized box labeled Team EverAscend Badges and handed it to Grace as he continued, "If you want peace of mind, take the reins and drive this rollout forward. Once you see how it works with the team, I'm sure your doubts will fade."

Grace's badges heated up slightly as she reflected on Victor's words. *Victor's right about one thing—I've always been a quick mover. That's what got me here, isn't it? But what happens if this time, moving too fast ruins everything?*

Victor interrupted her thoughts. "I think that's all for now, Grace. You can head back to work while I finish up here." With a determined look, he continued, "The whole industry is watching, Grace. Let's make sure they see leadership in action—not hesitation."

She nodded with an uneasy smile, waved goodbye, and left the lab to head back to her office.

When Grace arrived at her office, she closed the door behind her and leaned against it as if she could block out the anxiety. She glanced at her desk, where her unopened laptop waited and a garden salad and bottled water sat untouched. With her stomach in knots, eating lunch was not a good idea.

Take the reins, Grace. Take control. Her mind raced with questions. *What do I tell the team about the badges? About the project? They're going to ask for a plan—a real plan—and they'll expect me to have one. How can I lead them into something when I don't even know where it's headed?*

She opened her laptop, staring at the blank screen. *Maybe if I start outlining the project step by step... No, that'll take too long. What about focusing just on the first phase? But what if the team's ideas don't align with Victor's vision? I need to anticipate their questions—prepare for every angle.*

Victor's words, "The whole industry is watching," echoed in her mind. Her badges burned faintly, their heat pulsing against her skin like a warning. She clicked open a new document and began typing furiously, outlining potential deliverables and timelines, but the words seemed disjointed. Her fingers hovered over the keys, frozen. *I can't do this alone. But how can I delegate when I don't even have the full picture myself? If I don't stay in control, this whole thing will fall apart.*

Her phone buzzed on the desk, pulling her out of her spiral. She reached for it and saw Elliott's name on the screen. His text message was simple, direct, and timely: You weren't meant to carry this alone. Surrender. Listen deeply. The answers will come. See you tomorrow.

She stared at the text. *Control is an illusion. He's right, but how am I supposed to let go when everything feels like it's on the verge of collapse?* She responded with a quick thank you and placed the phone down, her hands trembling slightly. Taking a deep breath, Grace leaned back in her chair and closed her eyes. The badges pulsed faintly against her chest, their rhythmic energy amplifying her unease. She steadied her breathing as Elliott's words repeated in her mind. "Listen deeply and the answers will come."

A quiet sense of awareness came over Grace, and as she sat in the stillness, an image of her team flashed in her mind. She grabbed her notebook and flipped to a blank page, jotting down three headings: Team Strengths, Immediate Next Steps, Questions for Victor.

Under Team Strengths, she wrote Craig's name and circled it, adding *product genius* beside it. She remembered his meticulous eye for detail, how he'd once saved a client project by noticing a flaw no one else had seen. Tori followed with *social dynamo,* her infectious energy sparking ideas that turned even mundane campaigns into viral hits. Grace continued writing until each team member had their role and unique strengths acknowledged.

She paused at Immediate Next Steps, her pen hovering for a moment before she scribbled:

- Delay team badge distribution until I understand the tech

- Identify early signs of harm or changes in myself and document them
- Have strategic planning meeting with team for AscendSummit

Grace stared at the list, her gut twisting. She knew these steps weren't foolproof, but they were the best she could do with what little she knew. Protecting her team came first—even if it meant walking a fine line with Victor.

Finally, her eyes landed on Questions for Victor. Her pen paused briefly before she underlined *"J. Cain Initiative"* twice and added: "What is it? Why hide it?"

As she closed her notebook, Elliott's words lingered. *You weren't meant to carry this alone.* The chaos in her chest had finally eased, replaced by a tentative sense of clarity. She didn't need to have all the answers. She trusted that leaning into her team's strengths—and letting go of control—would guide her.

Her phone buzzed again, breaking the stillness. Expecting a reply from Elliott, she glanced at the screen and froze. A notification from her team's group chat glowed at the top: *"Whoa! Did you all see Victor's company-wide announcement? This is huge!"*

Her stomach tightened. Grace opened the app, her heart pounding as she scanned the flurry of excited messages. Someone had forwarded the email Victor sent out 30 minutes earlier—an email she hadn't seen until now. The subject line hit her like a slap: *"AscendGlobal Pilot Program Launches with Team EverAscend."*

She skimmed the message, her eyes catching on key phrases: "Our trailblazing team, led by Grace Stillman," and "demonstrating the transformative power of EverAscend 2.0 badges."

Victor had positioned her as the face of the initiative—without her knowledge. Worse, he implied that the badges were already being used by her team. Grace's breaths grew shallow as the magnitude of Victor's maneuver became clear. The clarity she had clung to began slipping away, replaced by a familiar knot of anxiety.

How could he? That wasn't leadership; that was a power play. What am I supposed to tell the team now? They're going to expect answers I don't have—again.

She took another breath and listened deeply. *I won't let this derail me. Victor's move was reckless, but I won't be. My team is talented, creative, and resilient. We'll figure it out together.*

CHAPTER 9

The Push and the Pull

Grace could barely get into the conference room before Tori ran up, practically leaping with joy. "So, Grace, what's the plan? This is so exciting. Victor said Team EverAscend is leading the way!" Angela added, "Yes! And finally, we'll get to use our..." she exchanged looks with Tori, and they both shouted "sexy new badges!" They laughed, Angela quipping, "Honestly, I think they deserve a runway debut. Fashion Week, anyone?"

Grace smiled warmly, keeping her tone calm. "Let's all get settled in and we can talk about it."

The energy in the room was palpable. Everyone was talking over one another—about the email, the badges, and the mystery project Victor had hinted at. Grace stood at the head of the conference table, watching her team with a mixture of pride and unease. Their enthusiasm was contagious, but so was their urgency. *They trust me to guide them, but how do I lead without steering us straight into the same dangers I'm trying to avoid?*

Grace took a deep breath. "Okay, team, let's focus. We won't take too long this afternoon because we have a full morning tomorrow. As you all know by now, Victor is announcing VirtuPath Vision 360 at AscendSummit in two weeks. A key part of the vision is the AscendGlobal pilot program, which includes premium Employee Achievement badges, Wearables, and Digital Recognition Boards."

She paused to let her words marinate. "This initiative will set the standard for workplace innovation—not just for us but for entire industries. Team EverAscend is at the forefront, and we'll be responsible for showcasing the potential of these tools. That means we have to plan carefully and execute with excellence."

Brandon interjected, "When do we get our badges? Victor made it sound like we've already been using them."

Grace hesitated, her mind racing. Grace looked over at the box of badges.

If I give out the badges now, I risk them getting distracted and, worse, being physically harmed by them. But waiting might frustrate them, especially with Victor's email already raising expectations. What would happen if I just gave them out now? It may not be so bad.

The urge to act was nearly overpowering.

Be still, Grace. Breathe. The answer will come. What approach will best maintain focus and minimize risks?

She smiled, her voice unwavering. "Team, you'll get your badges no later than Thursday morning, possibly tomorrow afternoon. I want us to spend tomorrow morning together working on strategic planning first so everyone is on the same page."

The team exchanged glances, their excitement tempered by curiosity. Angela asked, "Are you sure you want to wait? It sounds like everything is pretty urgent."

Natasha added, "Yeah, Victor's counting on us to set the standard. We can't afford to mess this up.*"*

John, raising his hand, said, "I can stay late tonight and begin working on anything you need help with."

Grace's smile softened. "Thank you, John, but I'd rather you go home to your family and get some sleep because we have a lot to work on tomorrow. And Angela, yes, it will be best to wait."

The room grew quieter, but Grace could feel the tension simmering.

Just as Grace was about to move on, Tori chimed in. "I have a few social media campaign ideas already—if we start tonight, we could get a jump on things. The sooner we start, the better, right?"

Several heads nodded in agreement, and Brandon leaned forward. "Yeah, Grace. We can split up the workload now and work until early evening. Then we can hit the ground running tomorrow instead of spending the whole morning planning."

Grace's badges warmed, almost as if they were feeding off her hesitation. The heat wasn't painful, but it felt alive, like it was urging her to move faster and give in to the team's demands. Grace began, "Okay, maybe we can—" and then paused. *No. That's not the way forward.* She took a breath and recalibrated. *This is exactly what Victor wants—us pushing forward and taking shortcuts without a clear direction. But how do I slow them down without killing their momentum?*

She continued, "I appreciate the enthusiasm, truly. But the best way to move forward isn't to jump in without a plan. We're going to take the time to align our goals and make sure we are intentional."

Her words hung in the air for a moment, met with a mix of understanding and uncertainty.

Angela crossed her arms, her voice tinged with impatience. "Grace, this is a big deal. Waiting feels... risky. Are you sure this won't set us back?"

Grace met Angela's gaze. "Yes, I'm sure," she said, firm but kind. "We're building something much bigger than a campaign, Angela. Trust me. This time, strategy and planning will make all the difference." She smiled at the rest of the group. "Thank you all for your input today. Let's meet here at 9 a.m. sharp tomorrow, ready to dive in."

The team nodded, their excitement still palpable, but as they filed out, Grace couldn't ignore the subtle hesitation in some of their faces. Back in her office, she spent the next two hours reviewing the AscendGlobal initiative, scribbling notes and ideas into her notebook. For every question she answered, two more emerged, but she found herself leaning into the uncertainty rather than fighting it. The rhythm of her work was different today—not frantic, but deliberate and purposeful.

As Grace walked to her car, her phone vibrated. She glanced at the screen and saw Elliott's name. The message read: "Leadership isn't about running harder; it's about walking wisely. Set the rhythm and the team will follow. You're doing great work, Grace."

She smiled and typed back, "Thanks, Elliott. Tomorrow, we'll start walking." She slid her phone into her bag, savoring the quiet strength the evening air seemed to carry.

The urge to control every step hadn't vanished, but it no longer gripped her tightly. There was freedom in surrender and pacing—not just for her, but for her team. They didn't need perfection; they needed a rhythm they could sustain together.

Tomorrow would indeed be pivotal—The path ahead was clearer now, but a quiet unease lingered. Something unexpected awaited them. Grace just hoped they'd be ready.

CHAPTER 10

The Tipping Point

Grace sat parked in her car for a moment, meditating on Elliott's words from the afternoon before: *"Set the rhythm and the team will follow."*

Today seemed critical. With Victor's email, the toxic badges mystery, and the press event at AscendSummit, finding the proper balance of setting the rhythm and controlling chaos was going to be key. With her laptop bag in one hand and the box of badges in the other, she stepped with cautious optimism into the conference room. You could feel the energy in the air, and the entire team was already seated at the table—display screen locked into its ready position and whiteboard cleared.

"Morning, Grace!" Tori called cheerfully.

"Good mor...," Grace began, but she paused, startled by what she observed. Tori was wearing a badge. *What the...?* One by one, she realized, everyone was wearing a VirtuVanguard badge, just like the one Grace had on her shirt. Everyone, that is, except Craig.

Angela noticed Grace's expression and grinned. "I know, right?!?! We look good, don't we, Grace? These badges are so gorgeous! Each of us found one at our desk this morning when we came in!"

Grace Under Pressure

Tori chimed in, "They were surprise gifts from Victor! Check out the note that came with it."

Grace read the note Tori handed her: *A gift to celebrate Team EverAscend leading the way. You're our pioneers. Let's show the world what VirtuPath can do!*

The EverGrace badge pulsed aggressively, matching her racing heart. *A gift to celebrate and motivate? More like a bold statement of control. He did this behind my back. What else has he decided for them without involving me?*

Brandon joked, "We're official now, Grace! Now all we need is Craig to join in the fun. Craig, where's your badge, sir?"

Craig shrugged, "I came here before going to my office. I'll go grab mine now. I don't want to be the odd one out around here!" He stood up to leave.

Grace's heart raced. *I can't let him put on that badge—but how do I stop him without tipping them off?* "Craig, can you stay, please?" Her voice was calm but firm. "Your input on the initial brainstorming is key, and we're getting ready to start."

Craig nodded, sitting back in his chair, though his curious gaze lingered on her.

The team's excitement filled the room, but Grace focused on Elliott's advice: "*Listen deeply.*" She inhaled slowly, closing her eyes for a moment and focusing on what she was hearing. The team's enthusiasm felt genuine, but something about it carried a restless edge. Tori's cheerful tone was just a little too bright. Angela's smile wavered as her fingers tapped against the table. And Brandon's energy, while contagious, seemed almost hyperactive.

Grace stood tall. "Alright, team, we've got a long but important morning ahead. Let's get started." She set the stage by sharing the vision for the AscendGlobal Initiative and their role in making AscendSummit a success. "Today, we'll focus on two items: first, getting early wins with the Employee Achievement badges for the pilot, and second, the logistics for AscendSummit, which is only two weeks away. We don't have a lot of time, but we do have the talent to make this happen."

Assigning roles, Grace made sure each person's strengths aligned with their tasks. The team dove into brainstorming, their energy channeling into productive discussions. Grace took mental notes, tuning into their unspoken signals as much as their ideas.

An hour in, Tori called out, "These VirtuVanguard badges are already helping us. It's weird—I didn't even need my usual second cup of coffee this morning. I just feel... energized, and I can't think of the last time we've gotten so much done in so little time."

Brandon added, "Yeah, I was planning to take the afternoon off, but now? I'm wired...like I don't think I can stop until we've nailed this all down."

John laughed. "How are those for early wins, Grace?"

Grace smiled softly. "Early wins are important," she said carefully, "but so is pacing ourselves. Let's make sure we're harnessing this momentum effectively. Angela, how about we recap and prioritize next steps before we wrap up?"

The shift in tone was subtle, but the team's energy began to stabilize, their focus sharpening. Grace exhaled quietly, gratitude for Elliott's advice filling the space where her anxiety had been.

Craig squirmed in his chair, "Grace, can we take a break now? I'm missing out on this VirtuVanguard productivity vibe."

Grace's body tensed up. *He's the only one without a badge, and I'd love to keep it that way. But how?* She turned to Craig, "Umm...hang on for another half hour, will ya? We have a scheduled break at that time." She continued to engage with the team.

Craig noticed her subtle tension and leaned over and whispered, "What's going on? Why does it seem like you don't want me to get my badge?"

"Let's step out of the room for a moment," she replied, her tone even.

Craig followed Grace out of the conference room and studied her with concern. "Grace, are you okay? You seem really tense."

She explained what she discovered in the technology lab and how the badges are more than just recognition tools—they are adaptive and influence the wearer's behavior. "Craig, these are not just badges. They are embedded with tech that is experimental at best and dangerous at worst. I don't know the details, but I did see a file or something called J. Cain Initiative – Phase 2."

Craig listened intently, his brow furrowed. "And you're saying that Victor knows this?"

Grace nodded, her voice low. "Yes, and he's counting on us to make this AscendGlobal pilot a success, no matter the cost."

Craig stood still for a moment, contemplating his response. "Grace, we shouldn't say anything to the team until we know more. Give me the rest of the week—just 48 hours—and let me handle this. I can analyze the badges, dig into the tech, and see what's going on. No need to panic everyone."

Maybe Craig can solve this quietly while I continue working with the rest of the team. Grace wasn't sure what to do. As she was about to agree to Craig's proposal, a strong thought came to her mind. It was more than a thought; it was a voice, and it sounded like Elliott. *"Take a step back and look at the bigger picture. What might this moment be preparing you for?"*

Grace reflected on the events of the past several days. *Keeping secrets is what got us into this mess. I can't afford to sideline the team for another two days—they deserve to know and can help find a solution.* She faced Craig. "I appreciate your willingness, but you can't—we can't—do this alone. The team needs and deserves to know the truth."

Craig frowned. "This sounds... big. Bigger than I thought." He ran a hand through his hair. "But if you're right—and I think you are—we can't wait. You're right. The team deserves to know."

The team was working diligently, and while Grace hated to disrupt the flow, she needed to reset the rhythm with the truth. She waited for Craig to return to his seat and cleared her throat. "I need everyone's attention. There's something very important that we need to discuss." The room fell silent.

Grace continued, "Before we take a break and continue with our morning, I need to tell you something I've discovered about the badges we're all wearing. The reason I have been holding off on getting the Employee Achievement badges to you is because I think they may be dangerous, and I've been working to see if that is true before alarming you. I wanted to protect you, but now that Victor has forced my hand, I think you all need to know."

The team focused on her intensely as she continued, "The short version is that these badges are embedded with microchips that Victor says 'amplifies ambition,' but what is happening beneath the surface is that the badges are aligned with the wearer's natural rhythms and supposedly fully adaptive. There is no transparency about the experimental nature of these and little to no concern about the side effects and physical impact to the wearer."

Tori and Natasha exchanged worried glances.

John broke the silence and said, "So are you saying that we are in danger wearing these?"

Angela crossed her arms. "Why are we just hearing about this now? We've been wearing them all morning. Craig, did you know about this?"

Craig nodded, his voice low. "Yes, but I just found out minutes before you did, Angela."

Brandon scoffed, "Grace, I think you're overreacting. This sounds a bit overblown, and I don't believe Victor would intentionally harm us."

This is harder than I thought. I can't blame Brandon for doubting—it does sound unbelievable. But this isn't about what's believable; it's about what's at stake.

Grace's voice was calm, yet firm. "Team, I understand that this is all quite unexpected, but we need to come together and figure things out. There's a lot at stake here and our priority is everyone's safety. Not just all of us in this room, but all of those who will be wearing the badges in the future."

Brandon had been shifting uncomfortably in his chair, arms crossed. "I still don't get it," he said, cutting through the tension. "We've all been wearing these all morning, and nothing bad has happened. Why are we making this into some big conspiracy? We're just talking about badges here. Celebration and recognition tools. That's it."

Natasha frowned. "Brandon, maybe Grace knows something we don't. Maybe we should listen…"

Brandon interrupted. "Listen to what? Some cryptic warnings with no evidence? Adaptive doesn't mean dangerous. It means smart." He stood up, "You know what? If it makes everyone feel better, then here."

With a sharp motion, he yanked the badge off his chest. The badge's magnetic backing clung stubbornly to his skin for a split second before tearing away with a faint, sickening snap. He staggered, his hand flying to his chest.

"Brandon!" Tori shouted, rushing to his side as he slumped to the floor.

The room froze. Then Grace's voice cut through the panic. "Craig, grab his badge and put it back on him immediately. Hurry!"

Craig quickly moved and picked up his badge and reattached it; immediately the bleeding stopped and the wound healed. Brandon, eyes wide and red-faced, sat up on the floor. He stared at his blood-stained shirt, speechless.

Grace knelt beside him, her voice reassuring. "Brandon, you're going to be okay. You may feel a little woozy and have some chest and shoulder pain for the next couple of days, but you're going to be fine."

Brandon met her eyes, incredulous. "Grace, what *is* this thing? I thought it was just a badge! What's happening to us?"

Grace turned to the anxious faces of her team, a quiet determination in her voice. "We need to stay calm and work together. Craig, grab a clean shirt for Brandon from the cabinet. Brandon, you can safely change your shirt when you're ready. Just leave the badge on—don't remove it again. Take off your shirt and put the new one on."

Brandon nodded, confusion and fear giving way to cautious trust under Grace's composed demeanor.

Angela wiped her eyes and said, "Grace, shouldn't we call 9-1-1 or something?"

Grace sighed. "I know this is scary, but Brandon's okay. I know because I've been through this myself. I didn't have the opportunity to mention that part yet. Or maybe I did and just didn't share it soon enough. I don't know. I'm sorry. This whole situation is hard." She was choked up, guilt trying its best to overtake her.

Craig placed his hand firmly on Grace's shoulder, meeting her eyes. "Grace, I can't imagine how heavy this has been for you. We've got your back, and we'll figure this out together." He turned to face the team. "So, what about you guys? Are we in this together?"

Tori immediately nodded. "If Brandon's in, I'm in. No question."

The rest of the team looked at Brandon, their expressions a mix of worry and determination.

Brandon exhaled heavily, his shoulders slumping. "Yeah, I'm in. I don't want anyone else going through what I just did. Let's do this."

This could've been so much worse. Thank God it wasn't. Grace mustered up as much confidence as she could. "Guys, let's take a short break. Go outside and get some fresh air. Grab some snacks. Do whatever you need to do. We'll regroup in 30."

Grace watched as the team quietly filed out of the conference room together. She waited until the last team member closed the door and picked up her phone to call Elliott. They were supposed to meet at the Willow Grove Café later on in the day, but she needed to talk to him right away.

The Tipping Point

"Hi Grace, what's going on? Are we still meeting later today?" Elliott inquired.

Grace's calm demeanor crumbled. "Elliott, this is a mess. My team is falling apart. Victor screwed me over by giving out the team badges before I could figure out a solution to protect them. Brandon ripped off his badge today in frustration, and we nearly had a medical emergency on our hands. We have the big press event coming up to prepare for and still have no idea how to handle this situation with the badges. I feel awful that I didn't keep Brandon from getting hurt. I should've told them sooner. I don't know, Elliott. They are coming back in 30 minutes for us to finish our meeting. How do I lead them when I'm barely holding it together right now?"

Elliott paused and continued gently. "Grace, you're carrying too much. Leadership isn't about holding it all together. It's about creating the atmosphere for the team to face this together. Collaboration isn't always easy. It often isn't. Sometimes it looks like letting your team see that you don't have all the answers so you can find them together. They trust you. Go lead them like I know that you can. You got this....and you're not alone."

Grace smiled. His words were like a healing balm for her rattled nerves. "Thanks, Elliott. Appreciate you always. Oh, and can I get a raincheck on our visit to Willow Grove?"

Elliott laughed softly, "I thought you might need that. Of course, Grace. I'm here when you need me."

She leaned against the wall, his words echoing in her mind. *Create the atmosphere for them to face it together.* Grace exhaled slowly, letting the weight lift. She didn't have to have every answer—she just had to show up and guide.

Grace stepped outside, letting the crisp air cool her thoughts. She spotted the team gathered in the shade, their laughter carrying across the courtyard. They didn't look like a group on the brink of collapse—they looked resilient. United. Her thoughts wandered to Caleb and Mia, likely immersed in their school day right now. Mia's smoothie experiments, always messy but somehow delightful, and Caleb's over-the-top tales of school drama…they taught her that leadership wasn't about control. It was about creating space for growth, for mistakes, for trust. She smiled to herself. *If I can guide them through the chaos of adolescence, I can guide Team EverAscend through this storm.*

CHAPTER 11

The Countdown

Preparing for AscendSummit: Two Weeks Out

Quiet energy filled the conference room as Grace stood at the head of the table, looking at her team. *This is the team that weathered today's chaos—and will get us through what's ahead.*

"Alright, everyone," Grace began. "Thank you for taking a beat outside earlier. I needed that as much as you did. But now, it's time to get focused. We've got two big objectives, and we're tackling them together. First, we need to fully understand what we're dealing with regarding the badges. Craig and I will dig into the J. Cain Initiative and figure out what this technology is really doing and how we can mitigate the risks. Your safety—and the safety of anyone else who comes into contact with this tech—depends on it."

The team nodded, their expressions serious but determined.

Craig raised a hand. "I've already started working on it. There's something about Phase 2 protocols that seem significant, but I need more time to connect the dots."

Grace nodded. "Good. Keep working and let's meet daily to review any findings." She looked to Tori and Natasha. "You two are taking the lead on PR and communications for AscendSummit. Our messaging has to be on point—transparent but strategic. Highlight the innovation without endorsing the current iteration of the badges. We're walking a fine line here, but if anyone can handle it, it's you two."

Tori gave a thumbs-up. "Already on it, Grace. We've got a few ideas to workshop tonight. If all else fails, we'll just post cat videos and hope nobody notices the fine print."

Grace laughed. "That's perfect." She turned to John and Angela. "John, Angela—you're on logistics. We need every detail of the Summit's execution to run seamlessly. Victor won't compromise on his expectations, but we'll build flexibility into the plans to adapt as we learn more."

John nodded, already scribbling notes, but Angela frowned slightly. "What happens if Victor pulls another surprise move on us? Do we just roll with it?"

Grace smiled. "We'll plan for the unexpected. And when it happens, we'll handle it—together. That's what we do."

Angela relaxed slightly, nodding her agreement.

Finally, Grace turned to Brandon, who had been uncharacteristically quiet. "Brandon, your insights are always sharp. I need you to work with Natasha and Tori on some external strategies. Keep an ear to the ground on how this is playing outside our walls."

Brandon gave a small grin. "You got it, boss."

Grace leaned forward, resting her hands on the table. "Here's the bottom line: we've faced unexpected challenges before, and we've come out stronger every time. This is no different. It's going to take everything we've got, but I know this team is up to it. We've got two weeks. Let's make it happen." The team nodded and went to work.

The Turning Point: One Week Left

Nervous energy lingered in the conference room. Grace noticed Craig fidgeting. The rest of the team was sitting quietly, scrolling on their phones, sipping on coffee, or scribbling notes. "Alright," she said, breaking the silence. "Let's figure out where we stand and what needs to happen next. Craig, let's start with you."

Craig's voice was low but firm as he began. "We're not dealing with recognition badges anymore. This is something much bigger than I originally thought—and much more dangerous."

The team exchanged glances as he continued. "I've been digging into the Phase 2 files from J. Cain Initiative. I don't know who J. Cain is, but whoever he or she is has made sure that these badges aren't just adaptive. They're collecting biometric data in real time—heart rate, brainwave activity, stress levels. That data is being fed into algorithms designed to predict and influence decision-making."

Grace sighed, "I guess that's truly what Victor meant when he said the badges amplify ambition."

Craig nodded. "It doesn't stop there, Grace. The badges have built-in mechanisms to manipulate emotional states. Long-term use risks severe mental and physical burnout."

Tori jumped in, "This would be catastrophic if we rolled this out globally. What was Victor thinking? He must know about this, right?"

Grace's brow furrowed. "I suspect he does, but it's hard to know for sure." *We're not just preparing for AscendSummit anymore. This isn't about presentations or saving face. It's about potentially saving lives.*

The team sat in silence, contemplating the implications of Craig's discovery.

Craig broke the silence. "If the public only hears Victor's polished narrative, we're complicit in covering up the risks. We need to somehow make sure the right questions are asked at the event."

Angela shrugged. "But how? We can't just walk into the press event and spill the beans. That is sure to blow up in all of our faces."

Natasha raised her hand. "What if we send an anonymous letter to key journalists—not to accuse anyone but to raise the right questions?"

Grace nodded. "Hmm...that could work. It's about protecting people, not creating drama. Subtle but clear enough to prompt a deeper look."

Tori added, "Exactly. We can focus on ethics and let them dig deeper."

Angela frowned. "But is this really the right move? What if the press twists our words or it backfires on us?"

Grace appreciated her caution. "I've thought about that, Angela. But the bigger risk is doing nothing. If we're honest and careful with our words, this letter could be the nudge we need to protect more than just ourselves."

Tori nodded, adding, "Maybe we focus on ethical questions—like the risks of adaptive tech going unchecked?"

Brandon slammed his hand on the table, the sharp sound reverberating through the room. "That's not enough! We need to hit them harder—make it impossible for them to ignore us. This whole thing could blow up if we play it safe."

The team froze, their startled expressions mirroring Grace's own surprise.

"Brandon," Grace said softly, leaning toward him, "what's going on?"

Brandon's knee bounced uncontrollably as he gripped the edge of the table. "Nothing," he muttered. "I just... I don't get why we're tiptoeing around this. These badges are dangerous, and we need to make that clear. If we don't—" He stopped abruptly, closing his eyes as if trying to steady himself, his chest rising and falling with each shallow breath.

"Brandon, breathe," Grace urged, her voice both soothing and resolute.

Craig leaned forward. "Brandon, are you okay? You're sweating."

Brandon waved him off. "I said I'm fine. Just… focus on the letter."

Craig sighed, his voice low but urgent. "This is what I've been talking about. These badges are manipulating us. Brandon's outburst isn't random; it's a direct result of the tech influencing his emotional state. It's amplifying stress, pushing him harder than his body can handle."

Grace met Brandon's eyes and held them steadily. She understood his frustration—it mirrored her own, though she couldn't afford to show it now. "Brandon," she said gently, her words measured, "what you're feeling matters. And it's not just you—it's the badges. This is why we're doing everything we can, including sending this letter. We need to stop this tech before it harms anyone else."

Brandon exhaled slowly. "Thanks, Grace. I just... I want to make sure no one else has to go through this."

Grace breathed in deeply as she turned to address the group and said, "It's okay," her tone firm but kind. "Team, let's take five, and then we'll come back to this."

The team reconvened and spent the next half hour crafting the letter, agreeing on a draft that raised ethical and health concerns about experimental adaptive technology without directly accusing VirtuPath of any wrongdoing.

Grace reviewed the letter and gave Craig the approval to hit the send button. "This looks good. I think it raises the right questions so people can think critically."

As Craig clicked the send button, a silence fell over the room as everyone exchanged nervous glances.

Grace leaned against the table, her arms crossed tightly. "It's out there now," she said quietly. "We've taken the best step we could. All we can do is wait."

The Stage Is Set: One Day to AscendSummit

With AscendSummit just one day away, Team EverAscend shifted into overdrive to ensure all remaining details were in order. The conference room table was scattered with laptops, empty coffee cups, protein bars, and notebooks. Grace cleared her throat and addressed the team. "Okay, we are down to the final hours. Remember our strategy is to remain innovation-focused but to steer clear of endorsing the badges too heavily." She turned to John and Tori. "John, Tori, you'll focus on finalizing the press kits and media briefings with the corporate comms director."

John nodded. "Already done. It was tricky, but I think we struck a good balance."

Tori chuckled nervously, "Yeah, I think we struck the right balance—clear enough to address the questions but careful not to overpromise or mislead."

Grace was feeling nervous but maintained a calm demeanor. "Since we already know that Victor is either in denial or complicit about the dangers of the badges, hopefully our anonymous letter to the press will be the catalyst we need to avoid a catastrophe." She looked over at Craig. "Any last-minute findings about the badges we need to discuss?"

Craig's tone was serious. "Let's just say I've discovered enough that if our anonymous letter strategy doesn't work, we need a backup plan because we absolutely cannot move forward with this pilot."

Brandon was quiet, rubbing his shoulder. "That's for sure. I know we'll all be okay since we haven't worn them for long. I'm just glad none of you are having to deal with the aftermath of taking one off."

The air in the room was heavy as the team considered Craig and Brandon's words.

Tori leaned over her phone, her expression shifting from concentration to excitement. "Guys, listen to this! Tech journalist Robert O'Neal just posted: 'Big claims, bigger questions. What's really going on at VirtuPath? #TheFutureOfWork.'"

The Countdown

Grace paused and nodded slowly. "Well, it looks like they're taking the bait. Let's hope it leads them to the right questions."

Grace's phone buzzed on the conference table, Elliott's name lighting up the screen. She quickly stepped out of the room, closing the door behind her.

"Hey, Elliott," she said, trying to keep her voice steady.

"Grace, how's it going? I had a feeling you might need to talk," Elliott replied, his tone reassuring.

Grace leaned against the wall, exhaling. "The team's holding it together, but I feel like we're balancing on the edge of a knife. We sent an anonymous letter to the press to nudge them in the right direction, but there's still so much uncertainty. And the badges... they're worse than we thought. It's a lot."

Elliott paused for a moment before responding. "Grace, you've done everything you can to set the stage, but now it's time to trust your team and the work you've put in. The outcome matters, yes, but how you show up—calm with a dose of humility and confidence to focus on what's right—that's what will resonate most tomorrow."

A small smile crept onto Grace's face. "Thanks, Elliott. I needed to hear that."

Grace reentered the conference room to find her team huddled around Tori's phone, murmuring about the journalist's post. As she stepped in, all eyes turned to her.

She took a deep breath. "Alright, team. We've come a long way in the past two weeks. I know it hasn't been easy—honestly, it's been one of the toughest stretches we've faced. But look at where we are now. We've tackled every challenge together."

She glanced at Craig and Brandon. "Craig, your research has been a lifeline. Brandon, your honesty and resilience remind me of why we do what we do. To everyone else, your adaptability, creativity, and commitment have made all the difference."

The room was quiet, but the energy shifted, a current of determination passing between them.

Grace paused, letting her words sink in as she scanned the faces of her team. Angela's worried expression softened, and Craig gave a nod of agreement. Tori offered a small, encouraging smile while Brandon straightened slightly in his seat, his earlier tension replaced with quiet resolve. "No matter what happens tomorrow," she said, her voice gaining strength, "we've already proven what this team is capable of when we work together in unity. Let's get some rest, believe for the best, and show up ready to lead. I appreciate you all so much."

The Countdown

Grace watched as her team prepared to leave for the evening. These weren't just coworkers—they were allies, united in purpose. Whatever happened tomorrow, they'd know they had done everything possible to stand for truth and protect others.

As the team filed out of the conference room, Grace sent a quick text to Elliott: *Thanks for the reminder. We're ready.* And for the first time in days, a spark of hope ignited within Grace—not just for AscendSummit, but for what lay ahead.

CHAPTER 12

Truth on Trial

The air hummed with anticipation as Grace stepped into the main auditorium at VirtuPath headquarters, transformed for AscendSummit. Minimalist yet polished, every detail spoke of excellence—from the dynamic VirtuPath Vision 360 visuals to the sleek LED stage backdrops and soft hues of blue and purple. Grace paused, inhaling as she absorbed the scene around her. This moment wasn't just about a press event or product launch; it was about courage, teamwork, and embodying grace under pressure.

Grace quickly met with Team EverAscend backstage to ensure everyone was clear on their assignments for the morning. "We will all sit together in the reserved seating at the front for Victor's presentation. Once it's press time, be sure to head to your assigned stations. Be prepared for anything because, as we've experienced, anything can happen. After the press event ends, we will meet in the Summit Room for a debrief. And yes, Brandon, there will be snacks and plenty of coffee."

Brandon smiled. "Good, because saving the future of work really works up an appetite."

Craig smiled and clapped his hands. "Okay, guys, let's do this."

Victor entered the backstage area and briefly greeted the team as he was pacing and practicing his opening lines. "This is the Future of Work, Team! Thank you for your hard work preparing for today. I know it was a lot, but you truly rose to the occasion. We'll talk more later. Getting started in five minutes."

Grace and the team nodded and headed to their seats.

The emcee warmed up the audience and called Victor to the stage. As the applause filled the room, Victor waved and smiled. "Good morning, everyone. Welcome to AscendSummit! I'm so grateful that all of you took time out of your full schedules to be with us today and hear about VirtuPath 360: The Future of Work!"

For the next 20 minutes, Victor delivered his presentation highlighting the vision of VirtuPath 360. The audience of experts, clients, and journalists responded with enthusiasm. In a surprising event, he invited Grace and members of Team EverAscend to the stage. "We have some real pioneers in the room. Without them, there would be no AscendSummit and no GlobalAscend pilot program. Grace Stillman, come on up here and bring the team!"

Grace, caught off guard, gestured toward her team, motioning for them to join her on the stage.

As they walked to the stage, Brandon whispered, "Sooo...do we smile, wave, or start an impromptu dance routine?"

The team laughed, slightly nervous.

Grace shared a few brief but heartfelt words, intentionally avoiding endorsing the badge technology. "Thank you, Victor. It's an honor to stand here with this incredible team. They have committed to a vision of workplace culture that is about more than metrics—it's about empowering people to thrive."

The attendees applauded as Victor wrapped up the presentation with his final remarks. "Thank you so much! I'll see you in 15 minutes at our exclusive press event. I'm looking forward to hearing your questions and diving deeper into what VirtuPath Vision 360 means for our industry and the future of the workplace globally."

Grace nodded at the team, and they exited the auditorium and found a quiet space outside of the auditorium to meet briefly.

Grace smiled. "Well, that was quite a surprise! Okay, let's make sure we are all clear on what needs to happen next. Craig, John, and Tori...you three will be with me. Brandon, Angela, Natasha...once things are about to get started, I'd like for you to strategically position yourself in various places in the crowd so that you can hear what people are saying and engage as needed."

Grace Under Pressure

The team nodded.

Craig leaned in and asked quietly, "Do you think the press will bring up...you know, the challenges we've had?"

Grace kept her tone measured. "I think so, but there's no way to know for sure. We've prepared as best as we can. Stick to the truth, stay calm, and we'll keep moving forward together."

As they entered the press room, they were met by a chorus of voices from industry executives, clients, VirtuPath employees, reporters, and other media influencers.

Tori scanned the room. "Wow, this is quite the setup! I'm going to grab some video."

While Tori captured social media content, Grace and Craig headed to the panel table that was set up in the front.

Victor walked through the side entrance hurriedly. He nodded as they took their seats. "Alright, team, this is our moment—let's show them what VirtuPath stands for!"

Grace and Craig exchanged glances as they spotted a few familiar journalists who are known for asking hard-hitting questions. *Deep breath, Grace. Deep breath. Stick to the truth. Everything will ultimately work out.*

Victor approached the podium, his smile confident. "You've seen and heard the vision for VirtuPath 360: The Future of Work. I'm eager to take your questions." Hands shot up across the room. Victor nodded to the first journalist.

Truth on Trial

"Victor, can you share specific examples of how this technology has improved productivity during your internal pilot program?"

Victor's grin widened. "Absolutely! Team EverAscend reported a 19% boost in productivity metrics within the first week of adopting the badges. They've been more focused and energized—a testament to what's possible. Craig and Grace can provide additional details one-on-one if you'd like."

The journalist nodded in appreciation, and another report shouted out, "What are the long-term goals for this initiative? Will it expand beyond corporate environments?"

Victor stood taller. "While corporations are our starting point, we see limitless potential. The initiative will eventually transform education, healthcare, government—anywhere people come together to work. Great question. Next?"

The next question hit harder: "How will VirtuPath respond if employees resist adopting the new technology? Is this mandatory?"

Victor hesitated for a moment. "Well...adoption takes time, and it's accelerated by inspiring enthusiasm through results. Everyone likes to win, and this technology helps you do just that—individually and collectively."

Grace sighed internally. *Inspiring enthusiasm. Not quite, but I guess that sounds better than enforcing conformity.*

Grace noticed the subtle tension rising in the room with the next inquiry.

"How do you address concerns that the badges' adaptivity crosses into manipulation?"

Victor paused for a moment too long before responding. "Adaptability offers a tailored experience for each user. It's about personalization, not at all about manipulation. VirtuPath's mission is Elevating Lives, Recognizing Achievement. Because Every Milestone Matters. Empowerment through innovation is what we're about."

A journalist's sharp voice cut through the murmurs in the room. "What is VirtuPath's response to rumors of health side effects associated with the badges?"

Victor's neck flushed. "We're not aware of any such rumors, but we're always open to addressing concerns as they arise."

The journalist pressed. "Would you like to hear the specific allegations we've received?"

Victor raised a hand, his tone rigid. "We're going to take a 20-minute break and then come back for any final questions. Please enjoy the beverages and snacks provided at the back."

Victor turned, his intense gaze locking on Grace. "We need to talk...now."

Grace exchanged a quick glance with Craig as they stood. Her eyes swept over the crowd, searching for the rest of the team. She met Brandon's and John's eyes and mouthed, "Let's go."

Craig sent a group text: *Victor might be losing it. Will text location of meeting once I figure out where we're going.*

Grace and Craig followed Victor as he walked swiftly through the side door. He turned to Grace, "What in the world is going on? Where did these rumors come from? This is an ambush. I bet our competitors are still sitting in that press room laughing." His voice lowered and was tinged with fear. "What do I do now? What do WE do, Grace?"

Grace had never seen him this way before. She looked at him, her emotions an unfamiliar mix of frustration and compassion. *He's terrified, and rightly so. But that fear doesn't excuse what he's done—or erase the fact that he's put us all in this position. Do we fix the press event, or do we finally fix what's broken beneath it? He might not like the answer, but we can't keep ignoring the truth.*

She finally spoke, her voice calm but with a hint of exasperation. "Victor, I won't sugarcoat this. We're in a mess, but the real problem isn't the press or the rumors—it's the choices that brought us here. If we don't face that, nothing we say out there will matter."

Victor gripped his temple and lost his composure.

Craig pointed to a nearby door, "Let's head into that private lounge." He gently steered Victor inside, and Grace closed the door behind them.

The press was waiting, but Grace knew the answers they all needed weren't on that stage—they were right here in this room.

CHAPTER 13

A Line in the Sand

Craig lingered near the door, his usual calm replaced by unease, while Victor's piercing stare landed squarely on Grace. "We have 10 minutes to figure out our next move. If we cancel the remainder of the press event, we'll look like we have something to hide. If I go back out there and refuse to answer some of the questions, we'll look like we have something to hide. This is looking like a lose-lose, thanks to this ridiculous smear campaign. Grace, what do you think we should do? Craig, you have any ideas? Jump on in here."

Craig looked at Grace, his eyes letting her know that he would follow her lead.

"Craig, please text Brandon to come to the lounge and ask the others to hang tight. Victor, we can figure out how to handle the press event, but we really need to talk about the bigger problem...the safety of these badges."

Victor looked confused. "What are you talking about? You didn't mention any safety issues with the badges. What aren't you guys telling me?"

Does he seriously not know about the badges, or is he playing games with me to try to cover his tracks? Grace gathered her composure with a breath, her voice calm yet unwavering. "Victor, I've been wearing these badges for weeks now, and it's taken a toll—physically, emotionally, mentally. It started small: minor aches, a warm tingling, and this strange sense of pressure every time I tried to slow down or rest. Then one day when I tried to take it off, the badge ripped my skin, leaving a deep wound until I quickly put the badge back in its place."

She watched Victor's face closely for a reaction. *I can't get a read on him.* She paused before continuing. "Then the same thing happened to Brandon. During one of our meetings, he ripped his badge off in frustration and collapsed immediately. Thank God we were able to get the badge back on him before things got worse."

Victor looked at Craig. Craig nodded, affirming Grace's story.

Victor's expression went from confusion to anger. "This is crazy, Grace. There's no way! Do you know how long I've been wearing all of these badges? Months, Grace. Months!"

Grace wondered how much longer Victor was going to keep up this charade. "Victor, since you're so certain that the badges can't harm you physically, try to take one of yours off right now." *This will call his bluff. He will make an excuse not to do it.*

Much to Grace's surprise, Victor took his hand and forcefully removed one of the badges. He immediately shouted in pain and instinctively replaced the badge in its place. The wound disappeared.

"Julian didn't tell me about this," Victor muttered, his hand hovering over the reattached badge. "This...wasn't part of the plan."

Craig, recalling their J. Cain Initiative – Phase 2 discovery, asked, "Julian? Are you referring to Julian Cain? Who is that?"

As if on cue, the lounge door swung open, and a tall, dark-haired man strode in with casual confidence, his presence filling the room. Brandon filed in behind him. Craig and Grace looked at Brandon, hoping for a clue, but Brandon shrugged, as he was uncertain who this man was who had successfully manipulated him into revealing Grace's whereabouts.

Julian stood in front of Victor, his voice terse. "Victor, we need to strategize. This press event is spiraling, and you've lost control of the narrative."

Victor's face twisted. "Forget the press event for a moment. What in the world is going on with these badges, Julian? Grace just told me about the harm they've caused. I just experienced it myself! Did you know about this? Did you know these things are *dangerous*?"

Julian raised a brow, his calm demeanor unshaken by Victor's anger. "Of course, Victor."

Victor froze, dumbfounded. "Wait, so you're telling me you deliberately made these badges harmful?"

Julian sighed, as though explaining to a child. "Harmful? Don't be dramatic, Victor. The badges contain a proprietary adhesive—let's call it Apexium—that interfaces with the wearer's skin and nervous system. It was designed to enhance focus, perseverance, and urgency. A temporary solution to ensure Team EverAscend hits every milestone."

Grace's stomach knotted. "You mean it manipulates people."

Julian shrugged. "Semantics. I'd call it enhancing performance. You'd call it manipulation. The results speak for themselves. Your team made brilliant progress in record time."

Craig's voice cut in, cold and sharp. "And what happens when someone tries to take it off?"

Julian's eyes darted slightly. "The adhesive forms a bond with the skin and underlying tissue—it's what makes the badges so effective. Removing them disrupts the connection, which can…cause discomfort. But again, these were never meant for long-term use."

Victor's face turned red with fury. "Discomfort? Grace and Brandon nearly passed out! You experimented on us—without consent."

Brandon lunged at Julian, but Craig stepped in swiftly, gripping his arm to hold him back.

A Line in the Sand

Julian waved his hand dismissively. "Victor, let's not overreact. The Apexium-enhanced badges were limited to this pre-pilot phase. The production-level badges will be far more user-friendly—lightweight algorithms, standard biometric syncing, and motivation analytics. No invasive tech, no adhesives. Just results."

Victor was trembling with fury. "We are supposed to be partners, and you used me! *You* put me in harm's way and made me the face of this...this lie."

Julian's smirk grew wider. "Victor, you weren't in harm's way—a leader like you, so attached to symbols of achievement? I knew you wouldn't take the badges off for months. And if you did? Well, the consequences would ensure you'd stay in line."

Victor paled, his hands clenched into fists. "You're sick. This goes against everything VirtuPath stands for."

Julian laughed coldly. "VirtuPath stands for *results*. All this talk of empowering lives and recognizing achievement—it's fluff for the press releases. What we're building together here, Victor, is truly the Future of Work. A future where human inefficiency is a thing of the past. Phase 2 is just the beginning. Wait until you see what I have lined up for us to do in Phases 3 and 4."

Craig, standing at Grace's side, asked cautiously, "What exactly are Phases 3 and 4?"

Julian's tone grew darker. "Behavioral alignment at scale. Imagine a workforce where every decision, every reaction, is optimized for maximum productivity. No hesitation, no rebellion. Total synchronicity between human potential and corporate goals."

A sharp pang of unease shot through Grace. "You're talking about stripping people of their autonomy."

"Autonomy is overrated," Julian said dismissively. "It's the price of progress."

Victor stepped forward, his voice unsteady but firm. "No. This stops here, Julian. I won't let you turn my company into...this. You've gone too far."

Julian's smile faded, replaced by a cold, calculating glare. "You think you can stop me, Victor? You're just the face of VirtuPath. I'm the architect. Without me, you'd still be stuck pitching half-baked ideas to investors." He softened his tone and continued. "Now, let's go back out to the press event together, Victor, and I'll stand with you as we get this narrative back on track." He looked over at Grace, Craig, and Brandon with a smile. "Team, I cannot thank you enough for your contributions. Once we get through the pilot stage, Victor and I have some major bonuses lined up for all of you and the rest of Team EverAscend."

Victor was incredulous. "You are out of your mind. You're not going back to the press event, Julian. I'll dismantle this entire initiative before I let you hijack my company again. Leave the building now or I will have you arrested and escorted out. My lawyer will be in touch with you shortly. Try anything stupid and I'll take this entire company down—and you with it."

Julian laughed. "Your righteous indignation is almost endearing, Victor. You wanted progress at any cost, and I gave it to you. Now you're too spineless to handle the weight of your own ambition. Pathetic. I'll leave now, but you're playing with fire. You think you have leverage, but I know every crack in this company, every weakness. Push me and I'll show you just how much power I really have." He stormed out of the lounge, slamming the door behind him. Victor stood in the middle of the lounge, physically and emotionally drained.

Grace walked over to him and gave him a knowing smile. "Victor, before we go further, I need to say something. I'm sorry I didn't come to you sooner about this. You deserved to know everything earlier, and I should have been courageous enough to have that conversation." She paused, then continued. "Look. I'm relieved that you didn't know about the Apexium-enhanced badges, but we need to talk about what you did know about and intentionally created—tech-enabled adaptable badges that manipulate employee behavior. Somehow you've convinced yourself that this path is the answer. It's not. You don't need the adaptable technology to make people better, Victor. Real leadership empowers; it doesn't manipulate. If you listen deeply, learn to trust, focus on setting sustainable rhythms, and collaborate with your team—those are tools that build something lasting."

Victor looked down for a moment, allowing Grace's words to wash over him. He finally looked up, his voice quiet. "I let this happen. I wanted success so badly, I didn't ask enough questions. I trusted the wrong person. By amplifying ambition, we weren't fueling greatness; we were creating toxic success." He looked over at Brandon and Craig. "I'm sorry, guys."

Victor straightened, his tone shifting from regret to determination as he addressed the team. "No more lies, no more damage control. It's time to rewrite this story—not with spin but with honesty. They may not forgive us overnight, but they'll respect the truth."

He placed a hand on Grace's shoulder. "Let's get back out there. This isn't over, but I finally see who I need to listen to, and it's not Julian—it's you. You've shown me what true leadership looks like. Let's go show them the same."

As they walked back to face the press, Grace felt something unexpected: hope.

CHAPTER 14

Epilogue

Ten Months Later

"I'll make you proud, Victor." Grace signed the agreements granting her 80% equity ownership in VirtuPath Inc.

Victor smiled, his tone confident. "Grace, you already have. You've done an incredible job during this transition phase. I knew this day would come, but I didn't expect it so soon. Still, there's no doubt—it's the right time, you're the right person, and we have the right team."

Victor leaned back in his chair, his posture relaxed. "It's been great to have some margin to explore new possibilities. I've been mentoring a few CEOs, and it's amazing to see them embrace a healthier approach to leadership. There's no shortage of hard-earned lessons to share with them." They both chuckled. "Seriously, Grace, your leadership continues to inspire me. I wouldn't have been able to make these changes without seeing your example. Thank you."

A knock at the door interrupted them. Victor grinned. "Hope you don't mind—I invited someone special to help us celebrate." He called out, "Come on in!"

Elliott stepped inside, his smile wide. "Congratulations, Grace! Or should I say Madam Owner and CEO?"

Grace laughed. "Thank you, Elliott. Or should I say Sir COO?" Her phone buzzed with a text from Craig reminding her about the upcoming Emerge town hall. Rising from her seat, she said, "Gentlemen, duty calls. Brunch at Willow Grove later to celebrate?" They nodded, and Grace made her way to her office.

At her desk, Grace glanced at the framed headline on the wall: *VirtuPath Under Fire: Innovation or Exploitation?* It was a stark reminder of the chaos that followed AscendSummit. Public trust plummeted as the media scrutinized the badges. #BadgeGate and #ToxicAmbition trended for weeks, while critics accused VirtuPath of putting profits over people.

Grace remembered the tough decisions they faced. She and Victor scrapped the AscendGlobal pilot and destroyed all Apexium-enhanced products. The internal investigation into the company's technology unearthed uncomfortable truths, but they used it as a chance to reset. The financial and reputational fallout was harsh, but owning their mistakes laid the foundation for rebuilding trust.

Elliott had been instrumental during that time, guiding the team through town halls, media briefings, and candid conversations with employees and clients. Together, they forged a new path for VirtuPath—one centered on transparency and integrity.

Epilogue

After the dust settled, Grace anticipated that he would resign from VirtuPath, but she was pleasantly surprised and grateful when he accepted her offer to move from operations director to Chief Operations Officer. Having Elliott wasn't just a win for the company—it was a gift to Grace personally. With his help, Team EverAscend had risen to new heights. Brandon was leading a new department focused on ethical innovation, and Craig was spearheading product development across multiple departments and was doing an excellent job helping the company grow in cross-department collaboration.

As Grace finished the final touches on her presentation, her phone buzzed. She read a message from Victor: *Hey Grace, just wanted to let you know—Julian's trial wrapped up today. The court convicted him on reckless endangerment and unlawful human experimentation for his use of Apexium. No deaths, thank God, but the medical cases linked to his "enhancements" were enough for a 15-year sentence. It's a relief to see some justice served, but it's also a reminder of how far we've come since that disaster. Julian's private investment in VirtuPath wasn't just financial—it was a stake in something far greater, and it nearly cost us everything. Thank you for leading us out of the mess he left behind. Couldn't have done it without you.*

She closed her laptop. It was time for the quarterly Emerge townhall event. As she entered the auditorium, she found Elliott waiting near the podium.

Grace Under Pressure

He smiled knowingly. "First town hall as CEO and majority owner. How are you feeling?"

Grace chuckled. "A little terrified, but mostly excited and ready."

Elliott nodded. "You've got this, Grace."

Grace stepped to the podium, her gaze sweeping the room. Victor smiled and gave a brief nod of support. Team EverAscend was standing together, watching with anticipation. Grace started her presentation—sharing updates on the company's progress, the lessons learned, and the new VirtuPath Emerge initiatives. She highlighted the Ethical Innovation Lab, which had already delivered tools like adaptive wearables that encouraged healthier work rhythms and the reimagined VirtuPath Augmented Reality (V.A.R.) interface, now a cornerstone for creative problem-solving and collaborative brainstorming. "The V.A.R. has gone from being a tool of unchecked ambition to one that inspires connection and innovation," she shared.

Grace also introduced the Recognition Through Purpose initiative, showcasing how the new wearable technology was helping organizations celebrate achievements in meaningful ways. "Imagine recognition systems that align rewards with employees' personal values and goals, making every milestone deeply impactful. It's already transforming workplaces," she said with pride.

Epilogue

Each word felt purposeful, each slide a testament to how far they'd come.

She shared her closing thoughts. "This company's past was built on ambition, but its future will be built on purpose. VirtuPath has been given a second chance—not just to rebuild but to lead in a way that's different." Grace smiled as she looked out at her team. "Our journey hasn't just changed VirtuPath—it's changed us. And now, our mission is to take what we've learned and share it with the world. We're here to prove that work can be meaningful, sustainable, and transformative—for individuals, teams, and entire industries. We're creating tools that cultivate connection, respect, and growth, not just within our company but in every workplace we touch. The ripple effect of our work starts here, with us. And I can't wait to see how far it goes."

The room was filled with thunderous applause. Grace looked out over the room, focusing on the faces in the audience—her team, clients, and partners. She thought about the hospital system that adopted VirtuPath tools to enhance collaboration between medical teams, leading to saved lives, and the school district that used the innovative recognition system and Wearables to celebrate teachers' achievements, boosting morale and student outcomes. This was just the beginning.

As Grace walked back to her seat, her phone buzzed again, this time with a photo from Caleb: him and Mia standing in the kitchen making goofy faces while holding a plate of chocolate chip cookies. The caption read: *Celebrating our favorite CEO. Don't be late for movie night!* Her heart swelled. VirtuPath's transformation was something to be proud of, but her greatest accomplishment was learning how to show up fully—not only for her team but for her family.

As she settled back into her chair, the words she had just spoken echoed in her mind. *We've done more than recover—we've redefined what it means to lead, to work, and to care. The grind may have built the old VirtuPath, but grace has given it life. And together, we'll show the world a way forward.*

The Invitation

Grace Stillman's story at VirtuPath Inc. reflects the challenges many business leaders face today. Mission-driven leaders work to create immense value, but too often, they become trapped in cultures—personally and organizationally—where ambition turns into a master rather than a motivator.

VirtuPath's founder, Victor Graves, believed that "amplifying ambition," both within the company culture and through its products, would yield groundbreaking performance. Yet, as he later admitted during AscendSummit, "By amplifying ambition, we weren't fueling greatness; we were creating toxic success." Victor's awakening was a sobering reminder that unchecked ambition can distort even the best intentions, undermining the very success it aims to achieve.

Grace's role as manager for Team EverAscend eventually required her to confront the unhealthy dynamics she had unknowingly become a part of—and even contributed to. Despite its flaws, she saw the potential of VirtuPath, loving the company and its mission enough to not only challenge its harmful culture but ultimately take ownership of its transformation.

The Heart of Culture Transformation

A company's culture transforms only when its leaders do, and at the heart of VirtuPath's transformation were two foundational decisions made by Grace and Victor: to choose service over self and faith over fear.

Service Over Self

Victor's biggest challenge was his need to prove himself. Haunted by the failure of his previous venture, he poured his efforts into making VirtuPath a success as a testament to his resilience. His ambition influenced every decision he made and clouded his judgment, leading him to align with Julian Cain—VirtuPath's silent private investor and a master manipulator.

At AscendSummit, Victor faced the hardest truth of his leadership journey: his pride had been the catalyst for VirtuPath's harmful culture. The need to prove himself led him to put his ambitions above the well-being of his team and customers. Choosing service over self required him to confront his failures with humility and to commit to a vision greater than his own validation. Through this transformation, Victor committed to rebuilding VirtuPath alongside Grace and Elliott, guided by a renewed vision of leadership.

Faith Over Fear

Grace's greatest challenge was fear—an underlying force that shaped her decisions and actions. Fear of failure, fear of disappointing her team, and fear of exposing her own inadequacies held her back from fully trusting both her team and her instincts. Whether it was shielding her team from the truth about the badges or trying to navigate Victor's unpredictable leadership, Grace often felt trapped.

Her turning point came when she chose to lean into faith, guided by Elliott Hart's wisdom. Choosing faith over fear wasn't a single decision but a continuous process—one that required her to release control repeatedly and step into uncertainty with trust. Through faith, Grace discovered a quiet strength—not in knowing every outcome, but in trusting the unseen.

The Wisdom Keys of Culture Transformation

With Elliott's guidance, Grace uncovered four keys that shaped her leadership and VirtuPath's transformation. I call these Grace Gifts (pun intended) because grace is what empowers you—and your organization—to fulfill your purpose with ease and authenticity.

Peace Over Chaos: Listen Deeply for Clarity

"Sometimes, the starting point isn't something you do—it's something you hear or sense. Grace, you've been good at

listening to others as long as I've known you, but right now, you need to listen deeply. Not just to the noise around you or even to your fears, but to the quiet whispers—the ones that come when you're still enough to hear them." ~Elliot Hart

Answers are often readily available when we are willing to slow down, pause, and listen. Stillness is often mistaken for inaction, but it's a powerful practice of deep, intentional listening. In moments of overwhelm, Grace was tempted to chase temporary relief—distractions that felt good at the moment but left her deeper anxieties unresolved. These short-term fixes, while serving their place, ultimately failed to deliver the renewal she truly needed. By choosing stillness over avoidance, Grace learned that peace isn't the absence of pressure—it's the presence of clarity, gained through intentional quiet and reflection.

Rest Over Striving: Trust as You Move Forward

"Remember, your strength doesn't come from knowing everything—it comes from trusting what you're being shown, one step at a time. Quiet your fears, and listen. The rest will follow." ~Elliot Hart

These words became a compass for Grace as she struggled with moments of deep uncertainty—questioning Victor's motives, uncovering the truth about the badges, and preparing for the high-stakes AscendSummit. In those

The Invitation

moments, fear whispered loudly, but Grace chose to counter fear with faith and relinquish the illusion of control.

Her initial strategy with Victor was to manage his expectations while simultaneously trying to solve the challenges with the badges on her own. This left her trapped in a cycle of striving for solutions she couldn't find alone. Peace and rest are inseparable companions. Just as stillness brings clarity, rest transforms it into confident action. Elliott's guidance reminded her to let go and lead with the clarity she had, trusting that more would unfold in time.

Before the AscendSummit, Elliott reminded Grace that she'd done everything she could to set the stage and needed to trust the team and the work they'd done. Her willingness to trust helped Team EverAscend hit the bull's eye and thrive in highly complicated circumstances.

Rhythms Over Pressure: Lead with a Sustainable Pace

"Leadership isn't about running harder; it's about walking wisely. Set the rhythm, and the team will follow."
~Elliot Hart

VirtuPath's culture promoted urgency, driven by Victor's desperate need to prove he could rise from the ashes of his last business failure. This was only amplified by the manipulative ambitions of Julian Cain, whose selfish interests focused on performance at all costs.

The relentless focus on urgency and achievement set an unsustainable pace, prioritizing speed at the expense of meaningful progress. Grace embraced Elliot's wisdom, making sustainable work rhythms a key principle of her leadership.

Before AscendSummit, Grace intentionally slowed the pace, encouraging her team to focus on clarity and quality rather than rushing to complete every last detail. Though the team initially resisted, feeling pressure to over-prepare, Grace's measured approach helped them regain confidence and stay grounded. Her decision ensured they stayed energized and delivered with excellence. She understood that setting the tone and stewarding the pace wasn't just her responsibility—it was an act of care and vision.

Collaboration Over Isolation: Build Together With Honesty

"Grace, you're carrying too much. Leadership isn't about holding it all together. It's about creating the atmosphere for the team to face this together. Collaboration isn't always easy. It often isn't. Sometimes it looks like letting your team see that you don't have all the answers so you can find them together." ~Elliot Hart

Grace started out trying to shield her team from the dangers of VirtuPath's badges, believing she had to carry the burden alone to protect them. Fear of failure and pride whispered that showing vulnerability might weaken her

The Invitation

authority and lead to disaster. Her early conversations with Victor were tense, as she struggled to handle the conflict on her own rather than engaging in open and honest dialogue.

Grace eventually realized that true collaboration called for humility and honesty—admitting she didn't have all the answers and couldn't carry the weight alone. By choosing to be transparent and inviting her team into the process of finding solutions, Grace cultivated a spirit of unity, turning her colleagues from coworkers into true allies. Their individual strengths and collective vision enabled them to achieve far more together than Grace—or even Grace and Craig—could have managed on their own.

When Grace let go of the need to control the narrative or fix everything herself, she finally approached Victor with humility. That decision opened the door to courageous conversations and shared accountability. Together, they tore down the culture of toxic success and rebuilt VirtuPath into a place of ethical innovation, transparency, and sustainability.

Now...It's Your Turn

"The grind may have built the old VirtuPath, but grace has given it life." ~Grace Stillman

In the world of business, the grind often earns you a badge of honor—a symbol of endless hustle and sacrifice. But as Grace discovered, it's a badge that comes at a substantial cost: anxiety, burnout, strained relationships, and missed opportunities for meaningful impact. What if you could trade that badge for something far more powerful—the ease and empowerment of grace?

Grace's journey shows how embracing peace, rest, rhythms, collaboration, service, and faith can transform a culture. How might these principles redefine your own leadership? Imagine leading with greater clarity, inspired action, a sustainable pace, and authentic relationships—all rooted in trust and a commitment to serving others. What small shifts can you make today?

Visit **YourIdealCulture.com** to access the free resources I created to help you answer those questions and more.

As Grace Stillman says, "The ripple effect of our work starts here, with us."

Start today by making one intentional decision to lead purposefully with grace—because the ripple effect begins with you.

~ Shae Bynes

About The Author

Affectionately known as 'Chief Fire Igniter,' Shae Bynes inspires and equips leaders to be catalysts for transformation in the marketplace. Authentic, bold, convicting, and loving—these are words often used by clients and peers to describe her profound influence.

With 25 years of experience that includes corporate leadership at a Fortune 50 company and more than a decade as a founder and full-time business owner, Shae brings a unique blend of insight and expertise to her role as a trusted business strategist and advisor to entrepreneurs and executives. A pioneer in the Kingdom business movement, she has impacted over one million people worldwide since 2012 through her writing, teaching, and speaking, helping leaders create thriving personal and organizational cultures.

Shae is a prolific author of numerous works, including her best-selling books *Grace Over Grind: How Grace Will Take Your Business Where Grinding Can't* and *The Kingdom Driven Entrepreneur's Guide: Doing Business God's Way*.

She holds a B.S. in Computer Science from the University of South Florida and an Executive MBA from University of Florida. Shae and her husband Phil live in the Fort Lauderdale area with their three beautiful daughters.

Made in the USA
Middletown, DE
14 February 2025